Museum Branding

How to Create and Maintain Image, Loyalty, and Support

MARGOT A. WALLACE

ALTAMIRA
PRESS

A Division of
ROWMAN & LITTLEFIELD PUBLISHERS, INC.
Lanham • New York • Toronto • Oxford

ALTAMIRA PRESS

A division of Rowman & Littlefield Publishers, Inc.
A wholly owned subsidiary of The Rowman & Littlefield Publishing Group, Inc.
4501 Forbes Boulevard, Suite 200
Lanham, MD 20706
www.altamirapress.com

PO Box 317
Oxford
OX2 9RU, UK

Copyright © 2006 by AltaMira Press

British Library Cataloguing in Publication Information Available

Library of Congress Cataloguing-in-Publication Data

Wallace, Margot A., 1941–
    Museum branding : how to create and maintain image, loyalty, and support /
Margot A. Wallace.
        p.   cm.
    Includes bibliographical references and index.
    ISBN-13: 978-0-7591-0992-6 (cloth : alk. paper)
    ISBN-10: 0-7591-0992-3 (cloth : alk. paper)
    ISBN-13: 978-0-7591-0993-3 (pbk. : alk. paper)
    ISBN-10: 0-7591-0993-1 (pbk. : alk. paper)
    1. Museums—United States—Management.   2. Museums—Public
relations—United States.   3. Business names—United States.   4. Brand name
products—United States.   5. Museum attendance—United States.   I. Title.
    AM11.W35 2006
    069'.068—dc22   2006011550

Printed in the United States of America

♾ ™The paper used in this publication meets the minimum requirements of
American National Standard for Information Sciences—Permanence of Paper for
Printed Library Materials, ANSI/NISO Z39.48–1992.

Contents

List of Illustrations

Foreword

It seems like a long time ago that marketing meant a nice brochure and a little advertising. We were businesslike, but the emphasis was on the "like." Today, of course, with competition coming from so many cultural and leisure areas, we need more. Creating a distinctive brand, and maintaining that brand, is a concept long known in other businesses, and now it is finally being acknowledged by our own.

Thinking of museums as businesses is a new skill. Today, as we market our product professionally, we have to define ourselves. And that's where branding becomes so important. More than a new logo or advertising campaign, our brand is our total interaction with the public; it defines and infuses every aspect of our museum, and makes us the superlative collecting, preserving, and interpretive institutions that we are. As each of us works, not just hard but smart, to maintain our businesses, the branding tool is essential equipment.

Branding is good business. It gives donors a set of guidelines for gift giving. It tells grantors why your museum is worthy of a grant. It pinpoints your contribution to the community in language civic and government leaders can quantify. As this book shows, branding is a business activity to be practiced by everyone in the museum who interacts with our many stakeholders.

A good brand helps a museum run more smoothly. Branding is good scholarship because it helps curators fine-tune their exhibitions and even write the labels. It is good education because it shows teachers and docents how to make the museum experience more meaningful. Branding informs community service because it is based on finding a niche in the greater culture.

In America, there are no small museums. We are a nation of big concepts and we are fortunate to have so many institutions collecting, preserving, and interpreting them. This book does an estimable job of showing how even small museums marshal big branding ideas.

Whether one represents a museum as a staff member, an administrator, a board member, or a supporter, everyone is part of the brand and can benefit from the examples in *Museum Branding*.

In my years as a museum president, chairman of the board of the American Association of Museums (AAM), and association board member, I have met many different museums—of every genre and size. Each inimitable brand makes the others that much more distinguished, and we all prosper.

Dr. Freda Nicholson
Former Board Chairman, AAM
Former Acting Director, North Carolina Museum of History
Former Board Chairman, Association of Science-Technology Centers
Former President and CEO, Discovery Place

Introduction to Branding

The Process That Turns Spectators into Loyalists

A brand is a distinctive identity that engenders loyalty. Branding consists of creating and maintaining a body of programs and attitudes that convey a clear promise, encourage familiarity, and generate ongoing support. Branding includes a logo and a theme, and then goes far beyond those items to encompass every activity that touches the museum's constituency.

Museums need a strong brand image because competition is tougher than ever. Every community boasts well-conceived, thoughtfully operated museums, each dedicated to meaningful subjects. Museums compete for visitors not only with other museums, but also with a worthy selection of cultural institutions from performing arts to libraries. Add to these magnets a slew of enticing leisure activities, from theme parks to jogging trails. Given a weekend afternoon with a little free time to spare, a prospective visitor has a tempting selection of destinations to choose from. Tourists, a staple of museums, also have many choices, and studies suggest that shopping is, in fact, their preferred activity.

More significant than the competition for visitors is the competition for donor and sponsor dollars. If there is one lesson branding teaches, it's that money follows the heart. Members join museums that satisfy their emotional appetites. Donors contribute to museums that enrich them in return. Sponsors support museums that match their goals. Branding a museum gives it an image and personality that supporters can identify with, and an institutional ally to whom they want to contribute funds.

Branding a museum starts with identifying its mission, a promise that every member of the museum family can agree with and adhere to. Branding continues when the museum develops a personality, a way of collecting and interpreting and talking that has a distinctive style. Branding becomes truly effective when all the museum's constituents hold the same indelible image of the institution.

Image is significant. A museum can define its brand, but it's the visitor and donor and volunteer who must see and feel the image. Branding pays off when, day after day, exhibition after exhibition, donor after donor, the image remains clear. Clarity and consistency are the hallmarks of good brand, one that stays meaningful and consistent at every touchpoint, or interaction, with the museum's constituents.

Good branding speaks about the mission and vision to all the people that a museum touches—its external and internal markets—in a voice that is distinctive and consistent. A consistent look and attitude help people feel familiar with the museum, and comfortable in giving it their loyalty. Branding reaches out in many ways—through collections, exhibitions, publications, marketing materials, Web site, partnerships, recognition awards, docent tours, store merchandise, programs, events, and signage—but always with the same personality.

Many museums speak of their loyal constituents—members, staff, and donors—as the museum family. These are the people who have chosen, among all other possibilities, to support their institution because it looks, sounds, feels, and seems like them. It has been said, you only have one family. In the best of all worlds, they have only one museum.

THE TOUCHPOINTS AND THE STAKEHOLDERS

More than just a marketing campaign, certainly more than a logo or theme line, branding operates at every point where a museum intersects with its public. These include but are not limited to:

- Collection
- Exhibitions
- Wall labels and panels
- Signs

- Education programs
- Education materials
- Brochures
- Membership and development materials
- Letterhead and business cards
- Web site
- Events
- Museum Store
- Café
- Annual report
- Publications
- Volunteer materials
- Building
- Sponsorships
- Donor wall
- Programs

The people who come in contact with the museum at these touchpoints are the stakeholders, a broad and diverse group that needs to distinguish your museum from all other cultural institutions with which they may choose to spend their time, invest their loyalty, lend their influence, and share their philanthropy. Here are a museum's constituents, the people with whom familiarity must be established and loyalty earned:

- Visitors
- Tourists
- Members
- Donors
- Patrons
- Sponsors
- Educators
- Corporate partners
- Curators
- Volunteers
- Director
- Staff
- Board of trustees

- Scholars
- Association members
- Guest speakers
- Community leaders
- Government officials
- Purchasers of store merchandise
- Diners at the café
- Vendors
- Media

The list may be incomplete, depending on the museum, and all museums are encouraged to regularly reassess their touchpoints and stakeholders.

2

Brand New Museum

Suppose you were suddenly given 5,000 artifacts and $5 million, and told to start a museum. There would be no requirements, other than the customary legal ones demanded by your community, state, and federal governments, and the guidelines proposed by the American Association of Museums.

From this starter dough, or pot, or attic—choose your metaphor—you must imagine systems of exhibiting; hire staff; outfit, renovate, or build a building; institute a visitor plan; design interpretations; develop a database of supporters; write a marketing plan; devise responsible ways to spend and invest the money; and name the museum.

Imagine that every day, from the moment your accept this charge, you will meet a neighbor, relative, coworker, banker, taxi driver, college roommate, child's teacher, the person sitting next to you at dinner, your letter carrier, the UPS driver, lawyer, colleague's wealthy husband, little kid in the car pool, the soccer coach, or a person sitting next to you on the plane—and each one might ask you: "What exactly is your new museum?" And you'd have to answer each one in a way he or she would understand.

Then, regardless what kind of a museum you describe, figure that someone will weigh in with how much they enjoyed the Gauguin (substitute any artist you wish) exhibition, their child's class trip to the pioneer's house, or the geode they got for a gift. Will you be able to explain how your museum is different?

As you progress in your enterprise, without even asking people for support, you'll hear apologies on the order of membership in another museum, season subscriptions to the symphony, and children's busy hockey schedules. How will you defend your cultural contribution?

■ ■ ■

A brand new museum needs a brand. It needs an identity that instantly communicates what it is, has, and does. A brand new museum needs a mission that informs its board and acquisitions. A brand new museum needs a personality, so people feel they know it, and are predisposed to like it. A brand new museum needs an image, which is how others perceive its identity and which helps in creating a reputation. Brand new museums need friends and supporters of like minds, who believe from the gut and the heart that this is the place for them. Brand new museums need exhibition designs and docents to help organize a visitor's journey through its exhibits. It helps if a brand new museum has a set of symbols and logos that tie all its materials, publications, programs, departments, and events together. A brand new museum may not have a store or restaurant or outreach program, but it needs a reputation so that when it starts adding features, they are readily accepted.

Of course, a museum doesn't have to be new to have a brand. All museums have an identity, personality, image, reputation, and some degree of fit with the people who will become its family and supporters. The purpose of this book is to help museums discover their brand, develop it to its highest potential, use it, and safeguard it.

If the fantasy of the brand new museum actually sounds real, it's because most museum professionals have already started down the road toward recreating their museum as a fresh, vibrant, forward-looking organization. Smart museums are finding their identities, articulating their core values, and as any good professional would do, seeking new ways to enhance their image. Just as new acquisitions are judged by their relevance to the museum's mission, new exhibition themes are tried and measured for the same aptness. With the museum's message in mind, new volunteers are trained to help interpret it and new audiences are solicited with the promise of a genuinely distinct experience based on that message. Everything from new acquisitions to new display cases is initiated with any eye to how it will enhance the existing footprint. Museum stores are expanded to include exhibit-themed merchandise. Restaurants and catering facilities are added to extend the museum's time with visitors.

All these activities, emanating from a basic mission and identity, are informed by branding. When a museum can claim a distinct identity from which it builds supporter loyalty, it has a brand. Branding has already begun in American museums and, as the underlying purpose of distinctiveness and loyalty becomes more ingrained, all museums will benefit.

Now, what should we do with all these crates?

The Indiana State Historical Museum captures the history of the state from the ground up. The mission is made clear before the visitor even reaches the entrance by the sculptural insets, representing phases of the state's history, such as agriculture, in the outer limestone walls. Photo by the author.

Exhibitions as Branding Tools

Content as Message

Every time a museum displays an object, it brands itself. Nothing so perfectly identifies a museum as its exhibits, and it is with these that the branding process begins. The collection, of course, is acquired according to the guidelines of the mission, and thus reflects the formal identity of the museum. Special exhibitions and traveling shows are also mounted to expand on the museum's mission. As themes are delineated and panels written, the personality and style of the museum start to take shape. These are the most visible, the most tangible aspects of a museum, the ones most likely to be seen by the public, and the ones on which a museum's brand image is built.

When exhibitions are first brainstormed, one of the first filters should be the branding test that answers the question: How does this exhibition reflect our mission and personality? Of course, a museum's collection will always identify the museum and reflect its stated mission. Theoretically, a museum could display any item from its collection and the visitor would understand the museum's goals. Usually, however, exhibitions are curated around a theme, and it is these narrations that distinctively reflect the museum's brand image.

For the largest museums, a stellar show is sometimes brand burnishing enough. For most museums, however, connections must be wrought between the show and the institution housing it.

Titles help make the connection. The name a museum gives its exhibition can be as quiet as a book cover or as flamboyant as a movie poster. Look at all the places the title is seen: posters in the reception area, brochures, ads, banners outside the museum and on street poles, tickets, fund-raising appeals, press reviews. Every stakeholder of the museum first learns about a new exhibition from its title, and holds that memory for years on items like catalogs, store purchases, or scholarly journals. The title can scream or inform, be pedantic or edgy; it will reinforce the museum brand a thousand times over. With e-mail messages now carrying exhibition names as part of the signature, blast e-mails will reinforce a brand even more.

Exhibitions influence the visitor's perception of the museum in every detail: subject, viewpoint, and time period covered; whether the emphasis is on the maker as well as the artifact; the number of artists and extent of time range; and the perspectives evident in the labels and wall panels. The layout of the exhibition also defines the brand: how objects are hung on the wall or displayed on pedestals; the style of frames; the distance between exhibits; the size of the labels and wall panels; the colors of the walls and panels; lighting; the amount of traffic allowed to flow through the exhibition; whether the exhibits can be seen close-up, from a distance, or at different angles; and the placement of an exhibition at the entrance, side, or rear galleries of the museum. All the signals that give coherence to an exhibition also send a message about the museum itself.

FLOOR PLANS AND GALLERY LAYOUTS

The organization of exhibition galleries is a huge subject, already handled astutely by curators, educators, and exhibition designers. What should be added to the discussion is branding: how the physical layout affects perception of the museum's brand. The route a visitor takes through a museum has its own semiotic. Some questions that might be asked are: How does a timeline versus a themed structure reflect our museum's image? Does a larger space or several smaller spaces help us communicate the museum's distinctive story? Do we want visitors to see the museum first, and then the special exhibition, or the other way around?

One problem common to museums large and small is the necessity of gerrymandering floor plans to accommodate tour groups, museum stores, and restaurants. Many an entrance has been relegated to the back entrance, or narrowed, or rendered less impressive. Functional changes can also change the meaning of a visit, a situation that can be corrected with supplemental signage that recreates in words what the entrance once communicated visually.

Sometimes the floor plan simply communicates the wrong message. Several years ago the Mark Twain House recognized that the successful author's beautiful home and furnishings did not adequately represent his lifelong dedication to social justice and pioneering civil rights activities. It misrepresented the iconic author's brand. To the Mark Twain House was added not only a museum with changing exhibitions on his social works, but "and Museum" to the house's name. This addition also accommodates a spacious welcome center whose function, in this case, aids the brand. Now visitors can be briefed before they enter the house and better relate the man to his home once inside. A new floor plan in this case restored the original message.

FIRST IMPRESSIONS COUNT

A museum's lobby is another area with brand problems. Often this neutral space dilutes or forestalls the message of the galleries beyond. Small museums have a distinct advantage here, as they can put their exhibits and their identity right at the front door.

A college museum that displayed its temporary traveling exhibitions on the first floor gave the notion that the museum had no collection of its own, no reason for students or other campus pedestrians to visit it more than once. For a brand to be accurately communicated, its mission can't be hidden in back galleries.

SMALL MUSEUMS IN A BIG POND

Many museums are part of a university, park district, or arts center, and it's hard to distinguish them from their environment. Sometimes it's difficult to identify them at all. Exterior signage and wayfinding graphics will help their buildings, and their brand, stand out. For instance, the sculpture placed throughout Stanford University's campus signifies the presence of the Kantor Museum of Art at the university. The Utah Museum of Natural History, Salt Lake City, Utah, places display cases right at the entrance, so even peeking through the heavy, gothic doors a visitor can see that it's a museum inside.

Finally, even a small space should be allotted for visitors—and donors, educators, and other constituents—to reflect at the end of the visit and let the brand sink in.

SUPPLEMENTAL PROPS

Whatever the exhibition, and especially useful with rental shows, there are many ways to infuse the museum's brand personality. Maps contribute local relevance and are endlessly fascinating to visitors; at a relatively small cost, they add a large dose of local pride. Costumes from a museum's collection can bring an exhibit to life, much the way a live docent can. Judiciously selected artifacts are wonderful devices for bringing individual detail to broadly conceived exhibitions. Docents themselves lend humanity, not to mention museum-specific information, to any exhibition. Historic Arkansas Museum proudly claims that no one ever goes into a gallery alone, a physical connection between the visitor, the exhibit, and the museum.

Exhibition catalogs and relevant books published by the museum should be flaunted near the exhibition. Verbally and visually they enhance the image of the museums in which the exhibition is held. A much less expensive printed piece is the simple notepad, printed with the exhibition name and museum logo. It encourages visitors to stop, reflect, and connect the museum's identity to the objects.

Music is an unsung hero in emphasizing the personality of a museum, cuing the subject matter or historical period of an object, telling the visitor whether this is a serious or witty object, and emphasizing the human maker behind an object. Music makes a strange place feel more familiar, an important beginning for establishing loyalty. Docents who go offsite to make presentations might consider taking tapes and a recorder to better connect with the audience.

Video can tie an exhibition to the museum and its mission. A few minutes of video, set up on a monitor at the entrance to a gallery, can describe the thinking behind the exhibition and reinforce the museum's goals. A taped introduction by a curator or educator who has a friendly voice, makes eye contact, and mentions the name of the museum establishes a relationship between the museum and the visitor. With a few modifications, this format could also be used for an "exit tape," played on a monitor at the exit of the museum, which summarizes the exhibition and its significance for the museum. Showing the human face of the museum reminds visitors of the institution behind the exhibits.

LABELS: CONNECTING THE MUSEUM TO THE EXHIBITS

The branding goal of any well-conceived exhibition is to connect it with the institution in which it is housed. The connection should be clear and starts with the museum's name and/or logo on labels and panels, audio guides, self-guided tour materials, study room tables, and coordinated merchandise displays. It's amazing how often and in how many places a museum forgets to "sign its name."

Most museums provide labels and walls that inform, and many imbue their exhibitions with all the writing skills of novelists, journalists, and screenwriters. Whatever the style of label, when deployed consistently it speaks with a distinctive tone of voice that helps brand a museum. The voice can range from scholarly through conversational to witty, and can be encyclopedic or discursive or concise. The style of writing will vary with the goals of the exhibition or the mission underlying the collection. In large museums or small, words on labels and panels and in scripts help the viewer connect the exhibit to the museum itself; they explain why the museum thinks its exhibits are significant.

Note that museums have many publics besides the visitor. Educators, donors, community leaders, and other stakeholders read labels to understand why the museum acquired the artifact and how it enhances the collection, or how an exhibition contributes to the museum's mission. Every stop adds to the perception of a museum's brand.

Labels can communicate in visual ways. The newest labels at the Utah Museum of Natural History are random-shaped slabs of brownish sandstone with a leaping antelope etched on. Visual branding is part of every label and sign, and often is as basic as the shape of the label, the color of the card, or the type font. Because these essential signs appear throughout the exhibition, they are subtle but powerful branding devices.

Labels can signify other museum attributes. Some museums tag their labels, where applicable, with a "Recent Acquisition" strip along the bottom. It conveys an energetic and forward-thinking brand.

There are few rules to writing labels and wall panels. Whatever their format or style, they will reflect the personality of the museum. How the artifact itself is described, whether it is placed in context with its times, any biographical information on the artist, and diagrams accompanying the text all convey an impression of the mediating museum. Some museums keep label text to a minimum, and that laid-back attitude conveys one brand image. Others print labels on colored cards that match the wall, showing a greater involvement of the institution. Still others stencil text on the walls or floor, further cementing the relationship.

Labels are a small museum's friend. Their information expands the significance of the individual artifact and the scope of the exhibition. The William Beith House, in St. Charles, Illinois, augments its labels with questions such as, "What do you suppose they used this for?" Visitors immediately forget the museum's size because their minds have been opened limitlessly. It is an excellent method of education that forms an enduring brand image.

A word about length. The only bad label is the overstuffed one, because the more attention needed to read a label, the less attention is paid to the museum. Excessive wordiness reads like a textbook, suggesting the information could be found anywhere. Also, all long copy starts to look alike. This diminishes the importance of the museum, and the visual charm that distinguishes the museum is overwhelmed.

Finally, the longer it takes to read a label, the shorter the quality time of the visit. People need to move around and engage in the free choice learning that is a museum's forte. It's the only way they can form an impression of what they've seen, and then reflect on their experience. This is how familiarity, loyalty, and brands are built.

The two Tate Museums in London pose a classic branding situation, and the labels do a powerful job of differentiating them. At the Tate Britain, paintings are presented as part of English culture and heritage: contemporary British literature, music, history, and politics are referenced on the labels. At Tate Modern, a different personality appears: all labels note where the artist was born and where he or she created the work, emphasizing the global, open border nature of art.

RENTAL EXHIBITIONS

When a museum rents traveling exhibitions, they should be chosen for relevance. Where the rental is simply interesting in itself, a crowd pleaser, then wall labels, an introductory gallery, or additional artifacts are needed to turn something merely pleasant into something meaningful. Wall panels are the easiest, with one or two paragraphs explaining the relevance of the show with the mission of the museum. If possible, artifacts from the museum's own collection should be woven throughout the exhibition, to bring it close to home and provide a local perspective. Budget and staff permitting, these artifacts might even star in a small, introductory exhibit at the entrance to the traveling one, demonstrating the parallels between the traveling show and the museum that is temporarily housing it. Bay County Historical Museum, in Bay City, Michigan, rented a Buffalo Bill Traveling Exhibit and added its own panels stating "Buffalo Bill stayed in Bay City." The connection was a Native American from the county who had been a member of the traveling show, and some of his memorabilia from a local university museum was integrated into the exhibit.

BRANDING OPS

Like photo ops, branding opportunities are quick reads, clear communications of what your museum is. Labels present many opportunities to enhance the museum brand, at the point that most explicitly defines the institution. Some fundamentals of branding via labels:

- Keep a consistency of label format. If you want a different design for each gallery, have a conceptual reason for each gallery's different look.
- Use distinctive graphics on your labels for visual differentiation. Labels needn't use expensive, original graphics. Iconic designs can be found in royalty-free graphics books, or in a museum's own literature. Label graphics include type font, color, and borders, as well as the logo.
- Write well. Avoid pedantry. Remember to woo the visitor and win his or her friendship. Then you win loyalty.
- Use large type. Many people will be reading over shoulders or from benches, and both scenarios encourage the kind of thoughtful engagement that builds brands.
- Place labels high on the walls, the floor, on stands, and at other unexpected places to make visitors stop and think. Museums' supremacy at storytelling stems in part from their three-dimensional and nonlinear structure.
- Utilize computer screens for labels or panels, and not just to project a tech-savvy image. Scrolling text allows for longer copy that the viewer can read selectively, a visual option similar to those offered by audio guides.
- Put artifacts with labels in the lobby, the restaurant, the museum store, the restrooms, the staircases, and the cloakroom. Even while visitors are

getting their tickets or waiting for friends, they're being introduced to and reminded of the museum's works. Small museums have no choice but to utilize their entrances (and exits), branding from start to finish. Visitors should never forget where they are or where they're leaving from.

4

Museum Boards

Carrying the Banner

Tax-exempt, not-for-profit organizations are required by law to have a mission and adhere to it, and it is the board's responsibility to assure compliance. From the legalities of governance flow a multitude of activities that support the mission and reinforce the brand.

Museum boards of trustees and their individual members are the leaders who will develop and maintain the brand, image, and mission of the museum in every area of endeavor. A valuable board member must understand the concept of branding; recognize the museum's constituents and competition; recruit, integrate, and train the right team of new board members; and develop a script of talking points for members to use when talking about the museum. Smart boards will form effective committees that stay on brand; select appropriate projects when planning benefits, fund-raising drives, and awards; and solicit wisely, especially when signing on sponsors. Because museums have so many stakeholders, boards must understand how to work with them all. The board will contract with donated services and vendors, meet the press, participate in community events, and deal with government officials.

Traditionally, board members are dedicated people who join because they like hard work and believe in community service. They may know law, finance, and museology. They probably are sociable, with many connections. They are respected for vigor and probity. Board members, current and prospective, because they are good businesspersons as well as loyal supporters, will catch on to branding quickly. The next step is to make them diligent brand stewards.

Explaining to the board the concept of "brand" is straightforward. A brand distinguishes one product from others in its category. It builds trust and loyalty with its stakeholders. Board types, because they're often involved with several organizations, tend to bundle their museum with all other cultural institutions. This is good for culture, but dangerous for individual museums. They must keep the museum's mission and image distinct. Branding is part of a board member's accountability. In fact, not-for-profit boards have a governance responsibility to explicitly state and carefully maintain a clear mission. Identity is not only good business, it's the law. And even though contemporary boards don't get involved with the day-to-day business of the museum, they do have to oversee ongoing adherence to the brand. Finally, the board must be reminded of what management and staff know only too well: museums are fighting serious competition from other culture and leisure activities; it's competition that has propelled branding to its current importance.

RECRUITING BOARD MEMBERS

Not-for-profit boards may or may not interview prospective members, but many rules of hiring pertain. In spelling out the job description and where they hope the prospect's skills will fit, they must also clearly delineate the brand. Since board members are expected to mesh budgets to mission, they need to understand what makes the institution distinct from all others. With a large part of the job devoted to soliciting funds, both public and private, board members must be able to talk brand. Foundations and government agencies fund organizations with a stable and distinct mission; individual donors want to identify with an institution, and need that institution to exhibit a clear identity. A board member is not only the steward of the brand, but its spokesperson.

When recruiting board members, the search committee should seek a range of talents and skills. Financial and administrative types are crucial for bringing organization to the museum. It is particularly useful to have board member with press contacts.

BOARD MEETINGS

After recruiting the right people, effective boards will utilize them well, assigning productive board and committee work, running tight meetings, and staying on focus.

Committees are one area where the tenets of branding sometimes disappear and it starts with the familiar words, "anyone's welcome to sign up for this committee." This kind of vagueness bodes ill for branding. Board members are selected for their specific talents, just as committees are formed for specific goals. Committee members should understand how each committee project advances the museum's brand. Casual droppers-in might not get the message.

Most boards meet five to six times a year and every meeting should count. Wherever possible, that means no rubber chicken lunches and no rubber stamps. The meeting should acknowledge the importance of the board members with a good meal and a participatory agenda. All meetings should feature updates from the museum staff and a review of mission. If news breaks between meetings, it's a good idea for the board president to contact everyone, preferably by e-mail, so they can discuss implications at the meeting. Meetings are the place to ask the question, "Are we on brand?"

At the first meeting of the year, the mission and brand should be reiterated and explained. Whoever writes the minutes is well advised to include the brand message. It will be a documented record of the museum's identity, not only for current members, but their successors as well, and is as important as the record of activity.

There are many activities board members involve themselves with, but in the interests of time and effectiveness it's best to home in on those that enhance the museum's brand and image. Recruiting members, planning significant fund-raising events, and soliciting funds are worthy uses of the board's time.

Although some experts feel that solicitations are the bailiwick of the development office, fund-raising rightly occupies some portion of every board member's time. It is essential that anyone who asks for money describes the product impeccably and knows the brand distinctiveness. If there's a tag line or slogan, it must be used accurately. Talking about brand is language that major donors will understand; it is terminology that makes business transactions more credible. Like any sales presentation, "the ask" should start with a carefully scripted brand message.

People on boards usually communicate well and, in fact, are selected for their ability to relate to the donor audience. A very few brand communication rules will sharpen their pitches. It's important to be direct. By keeping the talk short, the speaker won't be tempted to stray off message.

What the speaker says is not always what the listener hears, and it helps to ask for feedback, just to be sure the brand was identified accurately. Staying informed is essential so that any questions can be answered and understood in light of the museum mission.

Treasurer reports, annual reports, or whatever form your reporting takes, all need to be branded. The various governance bodies evaluate your financials against goals, and these can't be separated from mission. Also, everyone who reads these reports is also a consumer and will respond to your brand much as visitors do. The transition document also helps maintain the brand. At the end of the board year, as committee chairs assemble and organize their notes, they should note how each event reflected the brand. Once on paper, it becomes a template for branding that takes makes every subsequent board's job easier.

THE SERIOUS SIDE OF SOCIAL EVENTS

Not-for-profit boards are social entities. It goes with the territory and is one reason why a group of people who don't get paid can work together as a team. There will be many social occasions in the life of a board, and the fun works as a hardworking branding tool.

One of the first social events for board members is the preview tour. That first look at new exhibitions helps the museum reinforce the connection to the brand mission. When anyone asks a board member about the new exhibition, he or she can comment in a brand-intelligent way.

They look like parties, but benefits small and large—with their attendant publicity, promotion, and excitement—are disciplined systems for flaunting the brand. Everything from venue to menu can be created and evaluated for its contribution to brand communication. Since board members frequently assume the responsibility for finding a speaker or an MC, collaborating with local businesses, hosting media opportunities, printing the invitations, and signing the checks, it's their job to carry the brand banner through every step of the planning. About the speaker—or auctioneer, entertainer, or award winner—it will, of course, be a person who reflects the museum brand. Additionally, that worthy must be prepped about the brand personality and mission, and able to deliver a few brand-specific comments. The museum's distinctiveness can be described in initial correspondence and reinforced shortly before the event with a fact sheet or copy of the press kit.

Some of an event's suppliers may agree to do the work at a discounted price, or pro bono. While it might seem ungrateful to then stipulate adherence to the brand, this can actually make the provider's job easier. Having clear-cut guidelines prevents costly redos down the road.

The branding continues through the meal. Hosting a table is a board member duty that, despite its cost, is not a personal party. Invited guests should be the type of people who appreciate the museum's mission and can support the brand. They will be happy to listen when the dinner conversation touches on the brand and then, because they will tell their friends about the event, spread the word around. Smaller events such as lectures hold board members to the same standards; they serve as strategic occasions to introduce and explain the mission.

Art fairs, festivals, and other public events bring in new audiences, and when the venue, signage, booths, and speakers are all in sync with the brand, these events are as powerful as they are popular.

The same attentiveness applies to trips and tours. While it's relatively easy to stay on message with the destination—some museums go to art-heavy cities, some on whale watches—keeping every aspect of the trip consistent with the brand includes the pricing and the choice of hotels, restaurants, and sight-seeing. Every detail conjures an image, and sensitivity to branding helps select the right details. Some trips are organized to reward the board for work and philanthropy; some raise awareness among a larger audience; still others are training programs for staff. Whoever the stakeholder, trips are a gentle but powerful way to instill the brand.

Social events, for board members, include a lot of networking and their names are essential to the event's success. Name tags are definitely in order, as expensive as possible, preferably the kinds that are engraved on metal, so they look permanent. They visually identify the museum's brand, as well as you. It's the kind of small detail that supports branding at every touchpoint.

Another detail, not small but rather rare, is the photo op. If an event is fortunate enough to attract the media, everyone who might be photographed or interviewed should be prepared with a short response that includes the museum's name and the event's mission.

CHECKLIST FOR THE BOARD
How well does a board understand and implement its branding? According to one museum board member, if the following points are addressed, the board is on its way to good branding:

- Do we have a brand and can everyone define it?
- Who are our competitors, and what are their brands?
- Have we recruited and trained our board members well?
- Do we solicit with a coherent sales message?
- Do our events reflect our mission?
- Do our vendors and pro-bono suppliers understand our mission?
- Are we prepared to meet the press?
- Does every board meeting reflect and reinforce our mission?
- Do all our governance documents demonstrate that we have a brand mission and are adhering to it?

EVOLVING BOARDS AND NEW EXPECTATIONS

Museum boards used to be composed only of descendents of founding families. But with family members frowned on by accrediting commissions, new blood is needed all the time. New trustees bring an essential variety so the board reflects the community as well as the image of diversity that all museums want to project.

A manageable size for a board is twenty or more members, each of whom needs to be told upfront that they must attend all meetings, which usually total six a year. They should expect to serve on committees, meet and greet supporters, attend all events, and be ambassadors of their institution to the community. As for monetary contribution, the rule is give, get, or get off. Usually no quotas are set, and depending on the size of the institution, board member donations range from $100 to $400,000. Commitment of time and money begets commitment to the brand, and then total branding efforts can succeed. In seeking funding, board members should talk often about the brand. Foundations and government agencies give to organizations with a stable and distinct mission, and individual donors who want to identify with an institution need that institution to have a clear identity.

Boards should rotate after two terms so that nobody feels like the new guy, and anybody can be rotated off if they aren't contributing their part. Gone are the days when board members could serve simply by working on museum projects. The switch from a hands-on volunteer board to an administrative board is essential for professionalism, growth, and tighter governance. With the transition to professional boards, American museums are following the Europeans who were the first to establish professional directors. As museums around the world borrow from each other, borders dissolve and distinctiveness can blur. The many unique museums that make globe-trotting desirable will depend all the more on maintaining singular, individual museum brands.

LONG RANGE, SHORT RANGE, AND BRANDING PLANS

When mapping a museum's future, it's interesting that so many boards give it a chronological name. Unfortunately, Long Range Plans and Short Range Plans seldom include a timetable for building and instilling the brand. A good plan demonstrates how the museum's mission and brand can be strengthened over time.

Thinking about the museum's identity helps fit all the pieces of the plan together. It's a reminder that all long- and short-term activities are undertaken for a purpose: to further the brand's mission. At the same time that the conventional parts of plans are designed and implemented, their effect on the brand can also be evaluated.

Rising Schoolhouse, on the grounds of The Adirondack Museum in Blue Mountain Lake, New York, invites twenty-first-century schoolchildren to experience the stories of young people who have lived in the Adirondack region since the early 1800s. Courtesy of The Adirondack Museum.

5

The Education Department

Teaching the Museum

Visitors come through the doors in many shapes and sizes and degrees of willingness to learn, so the opportunities for meaningful communication are many and varied. At the same time that museums are interpreting their exhibits, they are introducing the museum itself and beginning a beautiful friendship.

Of course, museums reach most visitors through student field trips. These first trips, filled with new smells and sounds, new ways to socialize, new structures for the school day, and new people, not to mention new sights, are enduring memories. Field trips are wonderful occasions to begin branding your museum for the next generation of visitors; in fact, strong branding strengthens the educational experience. From pre-trip preview materials through the actual visit to post-trip follow-up lessons, the learning benefits from branding. Your first materials will give the museum's name and location, so students and parents know what's ahead. Preparatory readings or exercises give a flavor of the exhibits to come, and also a sense of the personality and mission of the museum. Follow-up lessons build on the memories that were begun on the trip.

In developing student field trips, docents will guide their school groups more effectively when they know where the schools are coming from, emotionally and culturally as well as geographically. That means knowing the neighborhood of the visiting school and how familiar its students are with museums. It helps to determine in advance the part your tour plays in the overall curriculum and whether tours are supplemental or fundamental. This is basic education programming, but also good branding because it links the museum with an already familiar structure. A corollary to finding out what need you fill is defining what benefit you hope the students will take away. Emphasizing benefits is another way to imprint the mission and brand of the museum.

It's not only the students who should be researched but the chaperones as well. Learning their experience and level of involvement will improve the success of the tour and the chance of making a strong branded impression. When guides know the other players in each day's program, they do a better job of weaving the museum's personality into the fabric of the tour. Advance information works both ways. When the schools have an idea of how the docents conduct the tours, it smoothes the way for a productive relationship between teacher and museum.

The teacher and chaperone(s) are your allies in branding. Their enthusiasm for the museum and its exhibits will help seal the students' approval. Calling them by name aids collegiality and puts everyone on the same side. A written sign, welcoming Mrs. Brown's class, is another way to recognize the teacher and make the students feel more at home and ready to learn. It also serves to introduce other people in the museum to the class, which will bring the teacher into the museum fold. And, it will force some good data-collecting habits on the museum's part. The properly spelled name, title, and school of every possible educator in town should be on your mailing list, especially if they've already taken the time to try your product.

Some museums ask the teachers and chaperones to help in teaching or cleaning up after the students. The former is better. Working together helps connect teachers to the museum.

Asking the teachers their interests and course load is more than professional politeness. It helps docents understand the importance of the field trip in teachers' schedules, both at school and in their personal lives. By discovering teachers' interests, hobbies, and special skills, the department can better adapt the tour and follow-up materials. When docents find common ground with their visitors and vice versa, it's another link in the connection. Of course, after hours, teachers are just adults who are prospects for membership.

By the end of the visit, teachers and chaperones should buy into the museum and everything it stands for. They will have had a stimulating experience for their students, a pleasant change of pace for themselves, and, hopefully, an involving introduction to the institution. The goal is not only making this field trip successful, but establishing a foundation for many future visits—by these teachers and their peers, either through the school or individually.

Branding during field trips or guided tours actually aids learning in several ways. By connecting the exhibits to the museum, docents give a structure to the exhibits, much as themes do. Branding helps tell the story of your unique museum and its exhibitions. For example, when Susan B. Anthony House gives students signs to carry on a mock protest march, learning activities and branding are merged. At The Adirondack Museum, teachers can reserve the Rising Schoolhouse and go about the school day much as students and teachers did in the nineteenth century. The museum provides pre-visit materials that describe the old school and suggest exercises that simulate a typical school day of 160 years ago.

These first trips, where future visitors, members, and donors first meet your brand, are a branding challenge, filled as they are with new sounds, new ways to socialize, and new structures for the school day, not to mention new sights. The branding starts quite naturally with pre-trip preview materials, preparatory readings, video, or exercises, and letters to the parents. All the preliminaries that strengthen learning also strengthen the image of the museum. Once in the museum, the exhibits and the learning program hold sway. This is where the mission comes to life, under the skilled leadership of trained guides. The personality of the museum is brought to life by the docents.

It's important to frame the exit as carefully as the introduction, and a smooth tour eases up to the finale. Don't take away the crayons or project sheets right away or funnel students into a dark coatroom: it suggests that when the visit ends, the museum disappears. A cheerful debriefing space helps the students discuss what they've seen or even act it out. A little energy expending is good. Too many chaperones enforce an orderly getaway when they should congratulate themselves that the tour has stimulated the children into so much activity.

At the end of the tour is when the reality is left behind and the memories start to form. Even the most stimulating education sequence will fade like exhaust from a departing school bus without follow-up from the museum. Before the field trippers ever leave, guides can ask students what they're going to tell their parents. This puts the visit in a familiar context and helps children recall their impressions. It's both a teaching and a branding tool, because it suggests discussion at home and ongoing reflection about their experience. Sending each student—and teacher—home with a memento of the museum aids the reflective process, and needn't be expensive. Be creative if you can afford it, but a bookmark with your museum's name is also a reminiscence motivator. It's always polite to say good-bye to the guests, by name, and invite them to return another time.

After the visit, a letter sent directly to the schoolroom, thanking the class for their visit, reminds everyone of the trip and the museum. The letter could thank students for asking such good questions, include some new information about the exhibits, and remind the class and teacher about upcoming events. It's both politic and brand-smart to copy the school principal, and so the list of contact grows. An important part of the letter-writing discipline is adding names to your database and starting a dialogue that, hopefully, will continue for a long time. Consider including a photograph of the class in front of the museum to connect the brand with the experience. This might be an even better time to send any supplementary video material.

Home schooling is casting museums in a new role, that of a major resource rather than a once-a-year supplement. For students without schools, museums become the place you have to get dressed for, where kids meet other people besides the family. Parents rely on not only the instructional material, but on the structure and stability of an institution. This trust is exactly what a brand wants its customers to feel. Strong branding, based on firm principles, will win the loyalty of homeschoolers, a not insignificant market that has the ear of other parents and teachers as well.

BRANDING OPPORTUNITIES FOR ADULTS

The adult docent-guided tour builds from a different dynamic. Adult learners have crossed the threshold voluntarily and are taking the tour with positive expectations. Ascertaining those expectations is an easier task than one might suppose if the docent simply chats a bit at the beginning of the tour. The docent should meet the group a few minutes before starting time to allow for a warm-up conversation. With a little rapport, branding starts automatically, and ongoing interaction firms the bond between visitor and institution. Again, the education process reinforces branding because it encourages reflection and retention.

Whether it's a children's school tour or an adult public tour, the only content-oriented people a visitor will meet are the guides. By whatever name they're called—guides, interpreters, or docents, they are the human face of the museum and many visitors will associate these persons with the personality of the brand. Some docents are selected for scholarship, some for teaching ability, others for people skills, and their effectiveness as branders starts with a branded training program.

The training manual, for starters, reminds docents why the museum needs them and elucidates the message they are to deliver. Many guides lapse into platitudes about the love of learning or the majesty of museums, but this happens only in the absence of information. Docents should be speaking to the specifics of your museum's exhibits and mission, and the manual is one place to state them loud and clear. If the training materials are too long—and length will vary by museum—they probably get into micromanagement. If docents understand the brand and mission, then they can be trusted with the spontaneous give-and-take that's so important to establishing relationships. The tone of voice of the handbook is as important as the details; scholarly or conversational, textbook or workbook, it sets the stage for how docents portray the brand.

The manual serves another function besides training: it's an internal marketing piece. Marketing to volunteer docents is a new trend, because for so long qualified volunteers were a readily available commodity in a world with few options to the local museum. Now, docents have busy schedules, at work and at home, and they need to be nurtured by the institutions they're supporting. This can be as simple as putting the museum logo on every page, so the rules have some context. Professionalism requires that the mission be stated at the beginning of the manual and repeated often. Respect for docents' intelligence demands that the manual be loaded with information, not just dos and don'ts. Many of the problems inherent in an instructional booklet can be solved by a good writer. If you think a training manual is too wordy, pompous, or boring, hire a writer and editor who can lighten it up. Just as they should read well, training materials should look appealing. They are part of the museum's image and docents are important constituents of that image. Their importance increases when one considers the wide circle of family, friends, and colleagues they influence. It's worth the effort to produce professional pieces for these valued, unpaid volunteers.

In any education program, the whole museum plays a role. The museum itself is the host and framework of the program and it's a good idea for guides to show a lot of it. The more exhibits or galleries walked through, the more chances of engaging a visitor's interest. Brand loyalty starts with affection for a few exhibits and develops into a bond with the entire museum. To create a sense of the whole museum, the guide can note recent acquisitions, talk about the architecture and landscaping, and supply anecdotes about the people who make the art and artifacts. The total picture covers not only space but time, too, so visitors might be told about previous and upcoming exhibitions. A museum has a full and rich story, one that helps attract and enfold all who enter. And it is a unique tale, so guides should be reminded to refer to the museum by name, the whole name. This is basic branding, because nicknames or generic names dilute the brand. It may be easier to say "this museum," or "here at the zoo," but it's proper to say the whole name and it also shows pride.

Given all the professional expectations placed on docents and guides, professional training might be considered. Some museums bring in presentation-skills coaches to improve docent presentations.

Museums educate not only through tours but also with lectures, courses, outreach programs, seminars, and videos. Each of these avenues brings people into the building and in touch with the brand. They present the museum in a format that's accessible to the nonmuseum-goer. Every time a newsletter or magazine arrives in a member's mailbox, they impress the museum's name. From discussion groups to professional seminars, adult programs greatly enhance the image of the museum, even if all the visitor sees is a sign in the museum or a mailer at the office.

BRANDING OPPORTUNITIES FOR FAMILIES AND TEACHERS

By sheer dint of entertaining their children on weekend afternoons, museums win the hearts of parents. They also win their allegiance with a hard-working variety of activity rooms, storytelling and vacation workshops, gallery tours, and children's courses. The next step is branded reminder materials. These could be as simple as the well-designed "passports" that let children check off the objects they see and earn a stamp at the end of the self-directed tour. Passports get taken home, another branding-plus-education tool.

Utilizing continuing education and professional development techniques, museums reach school administrators and teachers with a meaningful brand message. Well-branded marketing mailings alone convey an image of expertise and support. If it's a course, all syllabi and course materials should be printed on museum letterhead and organized in a folder with the museum's logo. The better designed the folder, the longer it will be kept and used like a store's shopping bag to impress all future fellow students.

Since the learners are in your museum for a longer period of time than the informal visitor who passes through the galleries quickly, they are open to your message and have time to contemplate it. It behooves everyone to take advantage of their presence.

You will never have a better occasion to meet your market, see how old they are, watch how they act, and study which exhibits turn them on. It's an unequaled opportunity to turn cold demographics into meaningful psychographics, to observe a target audience in action. And everyone in the museum can come out of their offices and join in the research.

Because interpretation is one of the defining features of a museum, education becomes a governance issue. Museums must state a mission and uphold it, especially in their education programs. When visitors turn themselves over to museum experts for learning, they are putting their trust in the institution and its offerings. Developing a mission, sticking with it at every touchpoint, and creating loyalty—that's what branding is all about.

Branding is in the details, like the iron fence surrounding the Edinburgh, Scotland, Writers Museum. Photo by the author.

6

Volunteers

Your Face to the Public

On a cold Saturday in February, a cheery middle-aged woman drives to a log cabin in a snowy Midwest suburb, builds a huge fire, pulls out her loom, and starts weaving. During the last week she has patched her shabby dress, ironed the petticoats, and reviewed her farm history. For the next eight hours this volunteer will move warp and woof to explain her museum to strangers. To her alone will fall the entire job of welcoming visitors, explaining the exhibit's purpose, and answering any and all questions. Except for the other volunteer who comes in once a day to bake bread on the hearth oven, no other museum spokesperson is present. She is the face of the museum. Of all museum staff, volunteers spend the most time with your public, who may well be prospective donors, community leaders, and potential volunteers. The weavers of the world are your first branders.

That's why it's so critical to recruit, train, and retain good volunteers, including those guiding tours, welcoming visitors at the front desk, answering questions at the garden hotline, or selling memories in the store.

RECRUITING

Whether recruitment is by word of mouth, referral, internal advertising, in newsletters, on the museum's Web site, or external advertising, qualifying the volunteer class is the first step. Busy staffers need some assurance that the applicant is serious.

If the process starts with a personal or telephone query, ask why the prospect is interested in being a volunteer. Is she a regular visitor? Does he agree with the mission? Does she want to help the community? Has he just retired? You don't have to screen at this point but note their reasons on the file you start for all applicants. Remember that you're looking for brand ambassadors, people who feel a rapport with the museum. Add all inquiries to your database; interested parties may not end up being volunteers but their interest could lead to memberships or donations.

APPLICATION

Regardless of the intensity of their interest, send application forms to all who inquire. The application should contain a serious questionnaire that helps you fit the volunteer's skills to your tasks. The form can be typed and photocopied, a multi-panel printed mailer, or an online form. It can be faxed, mailed, or e-mailed when completed. Make it long enough to require some serious thought and to impress the high expectation you have of volunteers. If it's too easy to complete, it's not a good measure of interest or abilities. Some of the questions can ask what is the applicant's vision or goal for the museum. Ask each applicant what kinds of talents, interests, or skills he or she has that might help the museum. Construct the application so prospects can see immediately where they might fit in. Volunteers should fit snugly so that they become the brand. While finding the fit, you also start to bond the volunteer to the institution. The questionnaire is not a weeding process but a seeding process.

Prospective volunteers have as many questions about the museum as they do about the job, and the questionnaire starts the dialogue. While you are getting a sense of the prospect's motivation, he or she will start thinking about the museum's identity and distinctiveness. An application questionnaire that probes an applicant's intent and, equally important, engages in a little soft sell might ask:

- How is Our Museum different from other museums in the area?
- What aspect of Our Museum is most important to you?
- If you take children to Our Museum, what do you tell them to expect?
- Think about an acquaintance who likes other museums but not Our Museum. Why would you tell them to give us a try?
- If you could change one thing about Our Museum, what would you do and why?
- Is there a museum in another community to which you would compare Our Museum?

- You have ten minutes to take a VIP through Our Museum. What would you show?

MEMBERSHIP

Once you've piqued their interest, lock it in with the requirement of membership. This will offset the costs of the training, such as postage, photocopying, binders, morning coffee, and evening snacks. More significantly, it underscores commitment and loyalty, the very traits you expect volunteers to transmit to visitors. It will help separate the shoppers from the serious volunteer prospects. The staff, stretched as it is, deserves a guarantee that the training time will be well spent. State the time commitment at the outset so volunteers will know their importance to the institution. If you aren't demanding some kind of monthly effort, you're asking too little; good branders need to feel like a meaningful part of the museum. Then recompense them with parking discounts and additional discounts at the gift shop, and you've started a solid relationship.

THE TRAINING PROGRAM

Depending on the volunteer job, training programs range from three weekends to one year. Smaller museums will find short but content-full programs perfectly adequate to their needs and available time-of-staff. Larger museums, with rotating collections and regularly changing special exhibitions, need eight to twelve weeks and periodic updates to cover the material. Several large art museums are famous for their yearlong docent programs that start to approximate a master's degree; this is part of their image. The volunteer training program is yet another way to reinforce a museum's brand, this time to the volunteer community.

For a docent, guide, or interpreter program, combine many different styles of learning in the training program, including slide presentations, reading material, team projects, independent research, and individual presentations. Vary the teachers by inviting curators, administrators, local historians, or artists to guest lecture. A museum brand is a rich entity, with many facets, and nobody minds too much instruction. Teaching a training session might focus the speakers' brand knowledge, too.

Plan on interim sessions to revitalize the volunteer corps, whether or not there's new information to disseminate. Because volunteers work alone, they seldom get to share ideas with each other, and the lack of interaction with their colleagues and the administration can distance them from the museum. They need refresher courses. A new exhibition calls for at least a two-hour lecture and walk-through. If you can bring in the artist, curator, or donor for a formal or informal talk, that will energize the learning. Use e-mail—or regular mail—to send appropriate articles on exhibits to all volunteers.

SHADOWING

Shadowing should be a part of all training programs. A kind of mentoring that business has used for years, shadowing assigns a new person to follow an experienced one. The shadower asks no questions and offers no suggestions. He or she simply goes through a typical day—or tour—with the professional. Not only is this excellent learning for new people but it also hones the skill of the regulars. Importantly, it also reaffirms your support for your veteran volunteers. Shadowing is a strong branding tool, one of the most effective ways to inculcate the institutional culture.

Practice runs, or dress rehearsals, also have a marketing angle. Encourage fledgling volunteers to bring at least one friend, at a time of their own choosing, for unmonitored practice. Practicing with a friend gives confidence, and new volunteers are always surprised at how much they know. It's good for the volunteer-in-training and excellent awareness-marketing for the museum. Nobody appreciates the museum brand better than a visitor who is guided by a friend.

Mark completion of the training with a certificate and a letter of acknowledgment from the museum director. The achievement deserves it and it is a form of internal branding—a tangible document. Check with local colleges to see if your course qualifies for continuing education certification or professional development units. This credential will help your volunteers who are teachers or students, and give cachet to the program.

If training is part of an internship with a college or university, that's a whole new branding opportunity. Many undergraduate and graduate programs combine curricular courses with professionally taught practicums. Colleges need you to develop the program, and you need them to supply a new generation of workers. That's fertile ground for branding and you should seek every opportunity to explain your distinctiveness from other museum internship programs. Guest lecturers, special student discounts and events, and Friday night open houses are ways to introduce yourself.

And now it's showtime; the volunteer is signed in and ready for duty. There's a good rule that your daily communicators should follow, borrowed from keynote speakers. It's the taxi-to-taxi rule that says: "You are on stage from the minute your audience might see you until the minute you disappear from sight." Not just when the speaker, or the volunteer, is "on."

Volunteers might be seen parking their cars, taking off their coats, or smoothing their hair. It's a reminder that everyone is part of the brand, especially to the people who buy a ticket. So volunteers should be at their posts before the visitors and, when leaving, leave gracefully. Conversation, in public, should be museum oriented. All volunteers will have name badges, the nicer the better. As for the rest of their attire, unless they're costumed interpreters, apparel should be understated. The museum is what's on view, not the volunteer's fashion statement.

RETENTION

No department wants to lose a volunteer, not after the arduous training session, and certainly not after the volunteer has become a valuable member of the family. These are the spokespeople who wear your colors, and their departure chips away at your image. There are several ways to "stitch in" your guides, to keep them in the fold. Assign them regularly and give them the work and discipline they signed up for. List their names on all correspondence and materials so they can get to know and support one another. Set aside a space for the volunteers' photos, brief bios, and a rack holding their name tags, so they see, as well as read, about their colleagues. Small museums with a volunteer corps of less than five people can team up with another small museum to share ideas. And, above all, stay in touch, through e-mail or regular mail.

Exposure to the decision-makers is high-level glue when it comes to retaining good volunteers' interest. Borrowing from current practices of corporate human resource departments, the director of volunteers might schedule occasional meetings where the museum director or chief curator can share information with volunteers. After all, even though they're unpaid, they're still working for the museum and they will do their job better if they are privy to new issues and goals as they occur. You don't need to tell volunteers everything that's going on, but talk about plans that volunteers logically have a role in supporting. Conversely, the administration can learn a lot from the knowledge of those who talk to visitors daily. These meetings are not social thank-you events. They have an agenda that's strictly business.

Schedule volunteer meetings in advance, even if you meet only twice a year, and send reminder e-mails in advance. Provide a written agenda. This looks professional and helps everyone stay on track. Part of the reason to nurture your volunteers is to keep them from finding a better social service activity elsewhere, so find out how other not-for-profits treat their volunteers.

FEEDBACK

Volunteers who have their heart in their work most likely use their eyes and ears as well, and they are uniquely positioned to pick up useful information on visitor attitudes every hour they're in the galleries. The questions and comments they hear should be disseminated to all the staff. With so many visitors coming from so many cultures and countries, it will broaden everyone's horizons to listen carefully. Feedback strengthens branding because a museum's image isn't just what it says, but what the public thinks.

The tour guide, store clerk, café hostess, or greenhouse worker can casually ask for comments or opinions, such as "Which exhibit did you like best?" Or "What will you tell your mom about this trip?" Encourage visitors to reflect on their visit and they will start storing memories immediately.

Docents, especially, should fill out comment sheets at the end of their tours. They aid the coordinators in formulating training and updating material. There's a branding advantage here as well as an educational one. When volunteers are asked for their advice, they feel more attached and become stronger ambassadors of the museum's brand.

A simple feedback system, to supplement volunteer notes, uses visitor comment cards. The cards ask for an e-mail address and states that the museum will respond to the question or comment as soon as possible. This is a wonderfully responsive system for tracking visitors' interests, helping to focus exhibits, keeping the staff in touch with the audience, and developing a database.

BRANDING TO THE INTERNAL MARKET

Volunteers are such an integral part of a museum's operations that it's easy to forget they are also consumers: visitors and members with a strong disposition to bring in family and friends. Although volunteers know the brand well, they might not think about it unless you remind them.

State the mission often, from the time of your first contact with prospective volunteers. Include the mission and personality in all your recruiting activities, whether by telephone, written pieces and ads, personal networking, or response to unsolicited inquiries. Have a positioning statement prepared that describes your unique identity. When you sign them on, emphasize that you appreciate their understanding of the brand and mission. Existing volunteers should be given a short, concise description of the museum to use when they are queried by prospects. Just as they deliver the brand message to visitors, they need to tell the story concisely to other prospective volunteers.

COMMUNICATE WITH LETTERHEAD, LOGO, AND PERSONALITY

Never send any communiqué or fact sheet to a volunteer that isn't on letterhead, logo-stamped stationery, or e-mail with a signature. Never go cheap with the people who are donating valuable time. Consider giving your volunteers museum business cards to use when conducting museum business. Cards may or may not carry the volunteer's name; what's important is the museum's identification. Volunteers might give them to visitors on tours, to vendors they go to for museum supplies, to customers in the store, or to contacts who want to be put on the mailing list. It's a relatively inexpensive way to help your volunteers be brand spokespersons.

Written materials should be concise, but that doesn't mean dry. Write with occasional bursts of personality and with examples where appropriate. Volunteers work too hard to be bored, or to think you're bored. Their written materials should be as thoughtful as the materials you create for visitors, donors, and sponsors.

For example, if you're explaining a pottery demonstration, don't just tell about the traditional techniques used. Tell a story about how "the Smith-Jones Museum investigated these traditional techniques to underscore the museum's commitment to understand Native American art." It's important to keep manuals relevant and interesting. From the branding perspective, you always want to elevate a generic activity, like a demonstration, to a distinctive museum activity. And mention the museum's name throughout. Even in talks to volunteers, formal or informal, frequently say the name. Museums, like people, shouldn't be referred to as "it."

To keep the museum's personality and identity alive, make it easy for volunteers to talk about it. Provide a lunchroom, or lounge area, for them to discuss the exhibits or share experiences. Even if they just linger a few minutes after their tour of duty, they'll be extending their involvement with the brand. And the friendships formed will create a stronger bond. Volunteers are good teachers for each other. Assign a mentor to new volunteers, someone who can answer questions, deepen their knowledge of the museum, and give them a sense of belonging. Though the museum only sees a volunteer several times a month, at most, these part-timers are probably talking about the museum much more frequently to family and friends. You'll help them spread the word by making branded materials such as brochures, ad reprints, and flyers available for volunteers to take home. Your workers are powerful word-of-mouth advertisers who are respected for their knowledge and insights. They have firsthand information, so it's no surprise that people would query them carefully. It's the perfect opportunity to hand-deliver your information and a good way to make the museum brand personal.

Now that you've gotten your volunteers warmly involved with the museum, comfortably projecting your brand, don't let them get too comfortable. Reinstruct volunteers periodically in the brand mission, which is more than the sum of its tasks, people, and assignments. The long-term goals are envisioned for everyone to see, and volunteers can help achieve them.

There's one short-term goal that lurks in the shadows of volunteerism: firing. In addition to absenteeism and incompetence, many of today's part-time workers have their own agenda. If they, in fact or by inference, hand out their own card at the end of the tour, they're taking attention away from the museum brand. Some museum experts recommend putting volunteers on one-year "contracts," so those who need it can be retrained.

Museums, large and small, are serious business, and training sometimes makes the whole enterprise too buttoned up. That would be a shame, a damper to inquiry and enthusiasm. So while it's necessary to dwell on one more rule, the dress code, let's lighten up. Literally, the volunteers should dress lightly, without too much jewelry, body decoration (that shows), or fashion statement. The museum will provide well-designed badges, with the museum logo, for all volunteers to wear. The rest should be basic bland. Some museums provide uniforms in the form of scarves, ties, or T-shirts. The Portland Art Museum goes several steps further by supplying accessories that reinforce the current exhibition. Thus, volunteers wore imperial sashes during the "Treasures of the Romanoffs," donned fezzes for the "Empire of the Sultans," and wrapped themselves in hapi coats for the "Splendors of Imperial Japan."

Whatever the nature of the garb, uniforms are recognized today for their many positive benefits, one of which is a feeling of belonging. The other advantages are a consistent look that reflects the museum's image, a ready identification of museum workers, and a sense of fun.

PERKS AND GIFTS

When it comes time to recognize volunteers, all awards or gifts should be branded. Whether it's a certificate for the wall, a discount coupon, or an emblematic gift, the museum's name will make it lastingly significant. At the end of the event, send the honorees home with a token of thanks for their family, reminding that background constituency about the mission that has taken so much dedication. Doing so can bring them into the museum family so they, too, can be ambassadors.

But don't wait for the annual appreciation day. There are other ways to your high regard can be expressed. If you attend professional conferences, consider taking along a volunteer. It's a large expense, and perhaps should be paid by the volunteer, but its value will reinforce the importance of your mission and the allegiance of people you want to retain. Alternatively, share information from conferences with the volunteers. Let them in on the knowledge that helps you achieve your end. If a conference is being held in your area, recommend that they volunteer to help at that event.

With small budgets and little time, museums depend on the kindness of friends. Gather your volunteers together for a field trip to a neighboring museum, to compare personalities and styles, and reinforce your own brand. In all endeavors, one learns a lot about oneself when he or she collaborates with the competition. Collaboration works wonders at uniting people, and staying in touch with volunteers if they leave for another institution is a goal to aim for. Many life events will tug good people from volunteerism, but their devotion to a brand they have supported never falters. Many will return, or send their friends, or apply their caring to another culture organization in another place.

Signature buildings are three-dimensional logos, and beautiful new museums bring attention to their communities. The Milwaukee Art Museum went deeper than international stardom and got down to basics with a pedestrian bridge connecting its lakefront location to the rest of Milwaukee, so that the celebrity building would be connected to the people and the communities who would use it. Photograph by Judi Schindler.

7

Membership

Converting Visitors to Loyalists

There are two ways to look at membership—acquisition and retention—and the means are quite different. To acquire members, you have to persuade and sell. To keep members, you have to remind and remind. Ultimately, what a museum wants is good members, those who will stay loyal. They're the best kind of member to have.

When convincing people to buy a membership in your product, you assure them that this new title, "member," will fit them comfortably. Good members (as contrasted with people who want cheaper tickets to the blockbuster or need to fulfill their charitable giving quota) feel a deep affinity to your museum. They feel so aligned with your mission, they wouldn't dream of switching to another museum next year. To acquire loyal members like this, assertive selling must be teamed with solid branding. When retaining members, you must remind them how much they have enjoyed the exhibitions, programs, and events. Then you remind them again about the museum itself, its mission and personality. You keep reminding them so they remember how your brand corresponds with their tastes. To retain members' loyalty, reminder advertising must be coupled with connection to your brand.

The mad scramble for members often obscures more important needs: signing members who will renew and upgrading members to donors. People who have been induced into membership with, say, a discounted blockbuster ticket, may not stay loyal. This is not to discourage museums from blockbusters, only to warn that they don't always produce long-lasting membership. The budget might be better spent on retention.

Once the decision has been made whether to promote to "blockbuster prospects" or "loyalty prospects," it's time to build the database. One database includes people who need to be constantly resold, people who joined to get inexpensive blockbuster tickets, liked the tote bag, attended a social event with a friend and felt obligated, attended a workshop through their company and felt pressured, or got a discount or special.

Members gained through these short-term promotions have immediate impact on your cash flow, but don't engender long-term commitment. They can be compared with people who clip coupons in the Sunday paper; they'll buy whatever brand is on special that week. They can be retained with more discounted offers.

Good prospects are people who attend several events over the years, join other cultural institutions, have children in schools that take field trips to your museum, eat lunch in your café, buy merchandise in your store, or reply to response cards in your newsletter or magazine. These people know your museum and what it stands for. They want to be part of it.

HUMAN RESOURCE DEPARTMENTS

Harvesting members individually is labor intensive; a more sweeping campaign can be waged with the third-party endorsement of corporate human resources departments. Forward-thinking businesses are finding that museum memberships for their employees boost morale, engender diversity, and provide the kind of enrichment that results in advancement. HR departments love museum programs because museum people know how to deliver adult education; they have programs that are universally accepted as "quality," and their offerings are affordable. Museums that have seen success with employee enrichment programs have expanded their presentations to administrative personnel. These upper echelon prospects are often missed because they don't have the leisure to fit museums into their agenda. Noontime programs, typically conducted in forty-five minutes to correspond with lunch hours, are effective because they reach targets through an intermediary that supports affiliation and loyalty.

Although your good brand name got you into the corporate office in the first place, you'll have to reintroduce it to your audience. As you describe your exhibits, explain your mission and let the museum's personality show. Tell anecdotes, give solid information, and edit your script carefully to waste no words because you have only the length of a lunch hour to convey what's singular about your museum. This might include the architecture of your building, a narrative about the collection, or even anecdotes that relate your mission with that of the organization you're visiting. People who give up precious lunch time to listen to a museum lecture are prime candidates for membership.

After the presentation, the speaker can leave reminders such as reduced-entry or two-for-one coupons, a calendar of events, or a bookmark with your logo. Without ever pushing for membership, the process has begun, and familiarity and loyalty will grow on its own. It is appropriate, however, to place a sign-up sheet at the door and add these names to your database for follow-up mailings.

OPPORTUNITY MARKETS

Office workers are just one opportunity market for members. Using a little imagination, it's possible to conjure up other segments that have not been identified by conventional classifications.

Summer interns at offices or resorts are good prospects: curious, young, educated, lonely, and leisure-starved young people. This group may be too temporary to warrant a heavy marketing barrage, but they'll be introduced to museums and that's a service for the whole museum community. Foreign students, airline personnel, and business travelers staying in long-term suite hotels are another market. As with all opportunistic campaigns, your strong brand identity makes the sale possible. It's easy for newcomers to understand what your museum offers, its value, and its applicability to them. The short-term results may pay off with word-of-mouth advertising and goodwill with employers.

Diversity markets have historically been difficult to locate because they live in many different ZIP codes and have diverse cultural activities competing for their attention. An African-American focus group, in discussing why they didn't visit a certain well-known local museum, said they didn't know what was there or how to get there. It turned out that no ads were placed in their local newspapers or on their favorite radio stations. No newsletters were sent to their ZIP codes. No banners hung from lampposts on streets where they worked. The constant brand image that is conveyed to traditional museum-going groups frequently doesn't penetrate through to diverse groups.

When reaching out to African-American and Hispanic markets, customized approaches are called for. Start by advertising in media that these groups use. They may not read the city restaurant and shopping magazines, nor listen to the classical music station. Publicize events through neighborhood churches, where much of the social life and a lot of weekend leisure activities take place. Family-friendly packages are particularly appealing to these cultures, and the makeup of the family may not be the typical mom, dad, and two kids. One African-American woman reported that as a girl she always took her siblings and cousins to the local art museum. Detailed driving and parking instructions, and perhaps garage discounts, are called for. In large cities, public transportation does not always travel in a straight line from ethnic neighborhoods to museum neighborhoods. Once a museum goes to the effort to identify diverse groups, and speak to their special situations, they will have created a relationship that branders dream of.

Branding to a diverse audience doesn't stop at the printed material. Take a look at your staff and make sure it is diverse. One of the best ways to create a personality for a museum is with people—the persons who meet visitors face to face. Newcomers of any background are somewhat intimidated by unfamiliar buildings, vastness of exhibits, and other visitors whom they always assume are more sophisticated than they. It's the job of information desk personnel, guards, and guides to put all visitors at ease. The recruitment effort that starts with advertising and promotion often succeeds or fails on the efforts of one-to-one selling.

SOLICITATION LETTER

Once you've captured the visitors that might become members, solicit them with brand-specific messages. Every museum fires off solicitation letters, discount coupons, gifts with membership, bring-a-friend promotions, and, at a higher level, VIP walkthroughs and members-only trips. The menu of membership perquisites has become generic. If you want your targeted loyal supporter to relate to your museum rather than another cultural institution, bring your brand to bear.

Start with the solicitation letter and write it well. When you talk about the history of the museum and its mission, talk in a tone of voice that's consistent with the personality of the museum. When you cite examples, tell little stories rather than list bullet points. Use vivid nouns instead of generic adjectives. If you mention, for example, birch bark canoes, carousing Flemish peasants, or whale oil, your letter will communicate more clearly than if you talk about "wonderful and unique" exhibits. When contacting existing members, remind them of the exhibitions mounted in the past year.

Instead of handing over the generic tote bag or mug with a logo slapped on, present a useful item that has meaning for the museum: a colonial-style teapot, gardener's apron, or pet food dish. Rather than categorize the giving levels by dollar amount, label them creatively as Prairie, Wetland, and Veldt, or Washington, Adams, and Jefferson. While other museums offer tickets for a friend, or the family, you give them a membership bonus for the whole herd.

PERKS

When member perks include a preview tour before the grand opening, or hors d'oeuvres with the guest speaker before the program, title these VIP events creatively. To get the ideas flowing, bring together people from different departments, including volunteers and interns. Remind them of the museum's mission, discuss the museum's personality, and encourage them to free-associate. At the very least this gives everyone a chance to think about what the museum means and to come to some agreement, an exercise in internal branding that is an accomplishment in itself.

Frequent-visitor programs encourage repeat visits and the continued involvement with your brand that leads to membership. The loyalty programs may, for example, after five visits grant the member a 30 percent discount at the museum store. Museums without stores can offer a perk usually available only to a higher level of membership. A frequent-visitor card will be in view for quite some time, so it contains not just the logo but a simple graphic to remind visitors not only of the brand but of the wealth inside. These graphics can be picked up from existing promotional materials.

TRIPS

A weekend visiting museums in New York, Fort Worth, or Minneapolis. Tours of famous English gardens. Day trips to private historic homes.

Invitations to the Masters Tournament. Wait a minute! Granted the side benefits of membership should be out of the ordinary, but if a destination doesn't relate to a museum, it doesn't qualify as a loyalty-instilling branding effort. If it's important to visit a place for its intrinsic appeal, rather than its relevance, a museum can follow the example of corporate incentive tour planners and book a meaningful speaker or conduct a short meeting there.

Membership reward trips can also be just plain educational, like outings for members' children, or working trips like those offered by environmental groups, or lecture trips. Membership benefits must be geared to every pocketbook, as well as to the mission and personality of the museum.

BRING-A-FRIEND PROMOTIONS

Sociability plays such an important part in museum-going that it's smart to devise promotions that encourage twosomes. Of course, all smart museums are using Buy-One-Get-One promotions (or BOGOs as they're known in marketing lingo) so it behooves each institution to adapt them to their own mission and personality. Don't offer merely a free admission for a friend. Offer a free admission for a friend to "take a safari to the Great Ape House with you." Don't merely request names of friends who might be interested in the museum. Ask for names of friends who "love western history as much as you do." Just as you want "good members," those whose interests will keep them loyal to the museum, so you want the same type of interests in their friends, and you can suggest the reasons why they might become loyalists.

Welcome the bring-along friend with special cordiality. Train people at the ticket entrance to note bring-a-friend passes and say, for instance: "Is this your first time at the Smith-Jones Museum? We hope you enjoy your visit." The same guidelines apply at the museum store, where bringing a friend entitles the bearer to a discount. Suggest that store personnel say a few extra words to the friend.

Mother-daughter events (or father-son) are a popular twist on bring-a-friend promotions. The old paradigm of family events still works, of course, and family programs increase membership, but there are new ways to define family that communicate your message in fresh ways. Mothers and daughters come in all ages and ethnic backgrounds, and if a museum has had trouble attracting minorities, or seniors, or working women, or corporate transfers, the mother-daughter approach could provide a new format for reaching them. There are many ways to communicate your brand to this segment. Theming might include mothers and daughters in art, mothers and daughters in history, or how science is addressing the needs of mothers and daughters.

Although there are ample senior tours and slide programs at senior residences, museums needn't stop at one-way outreach. Many seniors have the resources and the interest to become museum members, and it would be a disservice to underestimate their desire to contribute back to the community. As a group, seniors are highly brand loyal and meet all the criteria for being "good" members.

Membership is retention, rather than acquisition, of customers, and is a major goal of branding. It is easier to keep and upgrade the visitor you have than to keep advertising for new ones. Museums want visitors to follow up on the first visit and return. Then they want repeat visitors to follow up with a membership. And members become even more valuable when they follow up their dues with service to the museum, word-of-mouth recommendations, and donations. Follow through is the operative word.

Museums who want their visitors to follow up must do so themselves. It's an easy concept and a lot of work, because almost every membership activity deserves a follow-up. Member discount purchases at the store go into a database and get follow-up announcements. Bring-a-friend tickets collect names and addresses of the friends, who then receive follow-up promotions. Member previews or special parties don't end with the glow of a pleasurable evening: they follow up with an appreciative note, thanking attendees for supporting the museum. Of course, members receive follow-up thank-yous on receipt of their dues, and follow-up reminders when it's time to renew. Follow-up requires a maintained database and can be expensive in money and time, but it's the only way to convert and keep members.

The Grove

National Historic Landmark
Glenview, Illinois
(847) 299-6096

At The Grove National Landmark, its name is its promise. The main building is a log house, set amidst a very lush grove of sheltering trees. Its museum store is that rare retail space with a window on the rest of the museum, in this case through to the surrounding trees. It's a perfect example of brand reinforcing mission. Courtesy of The Grove National Historic Landmark, Glenview Park District.

8

Fund-Raising

Raised on Loyalty

Trading up is everything. The supreme advantage of branding is turning visitors into supporters, a ladder that rises to member, donor, and patron—from the casually interested to the dedicated people who give money regularly.

The ways of raising funds are as varied as pictures on U.S. bills: solicitation letters to members, benefits, events, in-kind gift, partnering, sponsorships, and naming rights. The creativity of the open hand ranges from collection boxes in the lobby to capital campaigns.

TARGET AUDIENCES

The target audiences can be defined many ways, too. As museums become more marketing-sophisticated, they slice the market more precisely. Some say go for the small but broad-based donors. Some insist on reaching for the biggest purses. One theory prescribes the middle, but steady, year-after-year donor.

Demographers are identifying a new sector, defined by age. People over fifty are now coming into inheritances. Individually these funds may not be huge but they are discretionary, and there are so many of them. Couple that with the high earnings of the baby boomers, and their proclivity to spend their money, not just hand it down, and philanthropy moves from wealthy men with wills, to healthy men and women with a will to help. Ethnic and minority groups in second and third generations support not only their own groups, but the larger community as well. And that's just the private sector. The business sector sees far-reaching value in partnering with museums and is approaching museums with the same vigor that museums are approaching them.

The reasons for asking for new dollars have also changed, commensurate with the growth of so many competing museums. Where once the funding was for a new gallery, acquisition, or staff person, now it could be for a more environmentally sustainable habitat or acoustically perfect auditorium. Frequently, prospects will have to be educated and they certainly will have to be persuaded. Donors need a clear picture of what they're paying for, almost an itemized bill of sale. Amidst all the variables of fund-raising, one principle emerges: you must clearly state your museum's brand.

With many organizations asking for the consumers' cultural dollar, choices will be made based on the museum people identify with; they've taken out the checkbook because they take a personal pride in associating with it. Fund-raising experts can walk a museum through the techniques of raising money. Only the museum itself can make sure the brand doesn't get walked over.

CAPITAL CAMPAIGNS

Small museums have a big advantage in capital campaigns: their single-minded brand image. Many potential donors will know the museum not as just a building with artifacts, but as an organic part of the community they live in. They know children who have visited there, people who work there, or others who have supported it. They know the museum's personality and they're sympathetic to why the money is needed. All museums need to position their fund-raising in this meaningful way. Three steps must be made, preferably simultaneously: identifying the need, creating a campaign theme, and appointing a message watchdog.

In a world of many capital campaigns, fund-raisers need a museum-specific reason for asking for the money. Donors have a plenitude of request for proposals (RFPs) in the inbox, from a variety of cultural institutions asking for improvement or growth funds.

A campaign theme is a rallying cry, short and dramatic. It's easier for a prospect to grasp "Save Our Courthouse" than a listing of whys and wherefores. This theme focuses the donor on a worthy cause, rather than a need. More significantly it focuses him or her on the museum itself.

Everyone in the museum is responsible for raising money, even those who have never asked for money before. A campaign theme keeps amateur solicitors from stumbling all over the subject, and the less-informed from giving incomplete information. A short, descriptive theme line helps the press write headlines, or reference the campaign in other community news. It also gives unity to the steady flow of announcements, reminder solicitations, and financial reports that should be sent. As posters, brochures, invitations, signs, and letters are developed, a campaign theme line ties them together. Costly marketing materials will go a lot further with a theme tying them together.

Having a campaign line doesn't guarantee consistency; a human being does. Regardless of the museum's size, there will be a multiplicity of communiqués, created by different designers and writers, aimed at widely divergent audiences. Also, a large campaign continues over many months or years, a calendar for mistakes that can be prevented by a watchful guardian of the message. Someone has to vet them and keep them on message. The message watchdog is a staffer or senior volunteer who peeks in everywhere, listens well, and has the standing to interrupt and correct anybody who strays off message. It sounds like a busybody job, and that's probably why it goes unfilled in most organizations.

All printed materials should be vetted by the message watchdog, everything from solicitation letters to speeches at Rotary meetings. Telephone marketing scripts should be cleared. Board members should be briefed and encouraged to use the museum's terminology, not their own. Curators and educators—professionals whose background gives them a vocabulary in their own field, but very few words for getting money from the public—can get a brief foreign language course in fund-raising. Even guards, guides, and store personnel need to talk from the same page, because the capital campaign will be a big part of the museum's daily life and the subject could come up at any time, from any quarter. And if outside grant-writers and professional funders are hired, they need to be relentlessly schooled in the specifics of the individual museum and its unique campaign.

FUND-RAISING EVENTS

Capital campaigns don't come along very often, but events are always available to double as development activities. Small museums, with their adaptable staffs, are very good at parlaying a small budget event into bigger fund-raisers. Brainstorming sessions, with all departments participating, can create events so novel that people will pay a premium to attend. For instance, a botanic garden brought in a celebrated chef to prepare dishes from heritage crops, and it became an annual fund-raiser.

A successful fund-raising event is any activity that (1) positions the museum in a new way, (2) reaches out to a new audience, or (3) is held at nontraditional times, such as in the evening or on Sunday morning. The idea is to gather in potential donors who haven't yet put you on their agenda. Novelty enhances the perception of the museum as a progressive, dynamic institution, and sheds new light on your story. Keep the novelty on brand, though.

The most tried and true fund-raising events become fresh when painted with the brand personality. A contemporary art museum raised awareness to new heights when it added a hot dog cart to its $150 a plate gala buffet. A museum consultant suggests sending gala guests home with recipe cards of the evening's menu.

History museums successfully conduct tours of private homes and gardens, new ones each year, which are rightly perceived as a privilege worthy of a special donation. These can be more closely tied to the museum's brand with a simple brochure pointing out how the period of the home, or its history, relates to the mission. Not to be avoided are signs placed at the front door or gate that identify not only the venue but the museum as the cohost. If the tours are guided, it's wise to prepare a script that threads the museum's name into the narrative.

Music concerts, by introducing noise to usually quiet galleries, put museums in a totally new light and raise money from new sources. The world of music is available to underscore a mission and a variety of formats as well. It could be a concert, a dance, musical games, or group bands or a solo performer.

Book readings and book signings are easy, highly brandable fund-raisers. Authors love the opportunity to publicize, sign, and sell their books, and benefit as much as the museum when there is a clear parallel. By providing space in the museum, the author gains prestige, as well as a larger venue. The museum gets a literary celebrity. The local bookstore or library can help line up authors.

Think carefully about the concept of the events, before you get mired in costs and logistics. Many a small museum bemoan the big bucks that bought a swell event but overshadowed the message. Conversely, solid connection to the donor pool is frequently purchased with a small budget and a clear brand concept.

OLD PASSIONS AND NEW FRIENDS

The donors you take for granted may not take contributing for granted. Don't rely on anyone staying on the list, or staying at the same level of giving. Keeping the passion alive is a daily to-do list, never a routine, that museums address with every exhibition, every item in the store, every tour. But unlike marriages or sports teams, a museum seeking passionate loyalty may have to find new audiences. Attracting new audiences could be the most important creative exercises a museum staff undertakes, because it forces an exploration of market segments you have never known. The place to start is with your existing audiences, and then expand.

For example, start with the students you attract for field trips and appeal to their teachers and principals. If you usually draw from a twenty-mile radius, use similar techniques to develop a following from thirty miles away. Think about the profile of your current visitors and then look for that kind of person among new residents to your community. Long-term "temporary" audiences are worth cultivating, and hospital interns, visiting professors, college students, and military families should be brought into the cultural community. Even out-of-town tourists can be "developed" into the family.

Sometimes new donors are simply old audiences with a different mind-set. For example, instead of targeting adults who are parents, target those same people as environmentalists or classic-movie buffs. Reach out to teachers at their home addresses, instead of at school. This could be the same old mailing list, but by appealing to a different motivation, you're actually reaching a different person. Museums are so well known they're overlooked; they have to break into people's routine to fetch a new look.

Timing is everything, and if a prospect hasn't given before, perhaps the time really wasn't right. Getting on people's fund-raiser agenda might be as simple as holding the fund-raiser on a Sunday morning, or at midnight. No reason why a zoo can't have a night owl buffet. The same creativity in timing applies to sending a solicitation letter or making a personal call. With most letters going out at the end of the year, a letter sent every Inde-

pendence Day might pull better. Personal calls to large donors at their
offices can get lost in the day's voice mail messages; a call at 8:00 a.m. or
5:30 p.m. often gets through on the first ring.

LOBBYING

Creativity is equally essential when applying for community or government funds. Just being a good museum isn't enough; a museum must
compellingly distinguish its contribution to the community's prosperity
and growth. Working from brand identity and strength, museums can
highlight their education programs, enrichment initiatives, services to
desirable new demographics, and attention to federal interest areas.

A good source for lobbying advice is the National Assembly of State
Arts Agencies, available on the Web at http://www.nasaa-arts.org/publica-
tions/advocate_strategies.pdf. The basics boil down to:

Don't focus on your program's details. Focus instead on the legislator's
interests and how your program—stating its name is often enough to
characterize it—solves his or her campaign on education, crime, or families. Show the effects of your program in towns throughout the county or
state, not just in your immediate area. Museums often have the reputation
of being elitist and out of reach of the underprivileged; you'll want to
change that image.

Once the legislators have delivered on their grant, invite them to deliver
the checks at museum events. To convert a one-time gift to a regular one,
show the lawmakers firsthand how important it was to the recipients. If
they can't come in person, nevertheless thank them at great length, which
can include a letter to the editor of the local papers. When public officials
appear at public gatherings of any sort, it's to show interest in the community and a go-getting museum administrator will be there, too. It's an
opportunity to network and share ideas on topics that both propound.

Museums aren't always asking for money and lawmakers aren't always
appropriating it, so stay in touch when not fund-raising. Send them the
museum's calendar of events, regular issues of the newsletter, and invitations to special program. Ask them to address your board or appear at a
museum conference. Loan them artifacts for their offices.

GRANT PROPOSALS

There's only one rule for success: know your brand, have a firm sense of
mission, and articulate it. Any one staff member who understands the

museum's mission has the ability to write a proposal and he or she should take a crack at it. Small museum staffers, accustomed to wearing many hats, are good at this. The reason so many proposals hit the wastebasket, according to executives in charge of corporate giving, is their failure to focus on the museum's individual, singular mission. They agree that articulating one's brand doesn't require the services of a highly paid grant writer.

PARTNERING

Volunteer-run small museums credit their associations with helping each other build strong events. At state and regional historical museum groups, proven ideas are adapted and new ones generated. It's not uncommon to pool resources and databases and share costs of campaigns. Partnering with a different type of museum doesn't lose members, it gains new ones. Partnering with like-branded local businesses or corporate underwriters also gains new money.

COHOST AN EVENT WITH LOCAL BUSINESSES

Invitees to fund-raisers love unusual venues and it may affect their decision to attend. There's a sense of privilege that comes from being at a retail store after hours, in a corporate penthouse, or a hardhat-only area. Unusual venues are not just clever party ideas, but good thought starters for sources of income. Imagine the audiences represented by benefits held at a hospital cafeteria, parking garage, water filtration plant, courthouse, nursery school, movie theater lobby, backstage, library stacks, factory floor, baseball field, locker room, or radio or TV station.

A fund-raising event that is supported by business lasts for a short time and ends. There is a one-time infusion of money, staff support, and shared mailing lists. A sponsorship continues over a long period of time. Not only is the financial support ongoing but the name association grows in value as the partnership is seen to endure. For the best chance of success, both brands must have similar audiences and goals, the museum's imprimatur must be prestigious for the sponsor, and the sponsor's brand name must be popular with the museum family.

ASSET-BASED DONATIONS

These in-kind donations build a museum. The guidelines of giving to the collection are a lesson in branding. By limiting artifact donations to items that further the mission, donors are forced to think in terms of identity and focus. The Wilmette Historical Museum, in Wilmette, Illinois, accepts only artifacts that were used in Wilmette households. The Ute Indian Museum store accepts artifacts from the Utes. The brand of the museum is clear.

Small museums tell wonderful stories with their exhibits, but they have to explain to prospective donors that donations will not always make it to the pedestal or the wall unless they fit a story line. Generous community members may not know about themes and may tend to think of their museums as encyclopedias. However, people don't give only from their attic and many are happy to ratchet up their donations with money.

ANNUAL SOLICITATIONS

Bringing money into the coffers brings people into the museum family and should be treated as a major branding opportunity. When people choose to contribute money to an organization, they're demonstrating affinity and putting their identity on the line. The museum, in return, gives them a consistent brand that never lets them down. While the intensive capital campaign creates excitement and attracts major gifts, the slow and steady, regular drive yields commitment. These small and medium funds underpin every museum because they reach a broad and diverse constituency, and make it easy for everyone to show loyalty. They have the advantage of frequent reminders. Every fund-raising letter, telephone call, e-mail, or personal contact must reiterate the brand image the donor has elected to support. The ongoing annual solicitation is an excellent tool for regularly reinforcing the brand.

BRANDING IS IN THE DETAILS

Everyone knows how to write a basic cover letter. However, "basic" is the antithesis of "branded," and sometimes the cover letter is all the recipient reads. The letter must be steeped in the brand. The first paragraph describes several activities of the museum that exemplify its personality: a recent program, new additions to the collection, or a research finding. If the mission statement isn't printed on the letterhead, the opening paragraph states it. If the museum has a tag line that goes with the logo, then it can be integrated into the letter or added at the end. A letter can be witty or serious, scholarly or informal, detailed or anecdotal. Once a museum finds its "voice" and its writer, it should keep them both. Trustees who write their own letters should follow the above rules, if possible, and if they're sending the letters under their own letterhead, include the museum's tag line.

The requisite handwritten personal note at the end of the printed letter should avoid bland clichés. "The new Courthouse and I thank you" is preferred to "Thanks for your ongoing support." The outer envelope and return envelope, which will join dozens of others in the week's mail, should also include the logo and theme line.

Telephone solicitations are treacherous territory for branding, so a script is essential for volunteer callers, and recommended for staff and directors. A basic thirty-second telephone pitch replicates the first paragraph of the letter, communicating not only the personality of the museum but enough detail to give the caller credibility. Callers should convey not only authority but sincere interest in the museum's goals. A major art museum likes to employ volunteers who are artists and designers.

E-mail solicitations, like telephone calls and letters, need to get to the point immediately, in the subject line. Make it attention-getting: "news from the Courthouse" becomes "gavel ready to pound at the Courthouse." Specific mention of an activity in the subject line works like a headline in a press release to deliver the message before a finger can hit delete.

Face-to-face "asks" need special attention because a real person, sitting two feet away, can overwhelm the unseen museum. Prepare a sales kit or leave-behind that the solicitor can use as a visual aid to focus on the museum. Even a photograph will bring the intangible to life. A high-impact prop, such as a brick from our hypothetical Courthouse, will help ground the discussion. Selecting the right person to make personal calls seems obvious, but easier said than done. The primary criterion should be enthusiasm and profound knowledge of the museum and its goals. Donors open up their wallets when they feel an affinity, and a sincere representative will provide the link.

DEVELOPING SOLICITATION LISTS

Regardless of the form of solicitation, nothing gets started without a database of names. Buying lists is not expensive, approximately $50 to $100 per 5,000 names, depending on the number of parameters. It's the postage that costs so much, and all the more reason to mine your data. Keeping track of who responds, with how much, is the kind of sophisticated fundraising all museums aspire to. For a system that's less high-tech, less-expensive, and more accurate, bring out the guest books and comment cards. Both should be placed at easy sign-up points in the lobby, coat check, café, and museum store. When possible, ask for the names of friends who might be interested. Of course, the guest book and comment cards must be proprietary—nothing store bought—with the logo, tag line, address, and e-mail large and legible.

Collecting names eventually becomes a habit, with everyone a list maker, and everyone else going on the list. Staff should be encouraged to jot down the contact of everyone who crosses their path: museum store purchasers and gift recipients, where available; café visitors; schoolteachers and chaperones who have led field trips; volunteer applicants; attendees at lectures and performances; guests at catered functions; vendors; and audiences at off-campus lectures.

LOBBY DONATION BOX

The lobby is where museum visitors receive their first impressions and absorb their lasting impressions, and assuming that these are good impressions, it is a good place to request donations. Donation boxes are rather passive ways to collect monetary gifts, but you can make these silent solicitors work hard. Since most museum visitors expect to pay for their visit, don't be shy about posting a sign asking for a token payment. Then make the request more brand specific. Instead of "Please contribute what you can" say "Your support helps build the Museum study center."

Place the donation box front and center, proudly. Keep it clean and neat by cleaning the glass, touching up the paint, and stocking it with crisp bills and shiny coins. Construct a box that's big enough to be seen, but not so big that it seems impossible to fill. You wouldn't send a shabby salesman to solicit funds and you wouldn't throw a cheap benefit party. The donation box, like everything else, reflects the brand.

Consider using the services of a designer so it looks like a part of the museum, not an afterthought. Build the collection box out of interesting materials—brick, birch bark, mosaic tiles, and textiles. Echo a shape or function of an artifact. The Serpentine Gallery in London has one of the best. It looks like an upright pinball or pachinko machine, where steel balls roll down a maze to the goal. In this case, the metal spheres are coins. It's a fun and creative donation box, reflecting the whimsical creativity of this contemporary art museum. With imagination and good craftsmanship, you can make the process of giving money an integral part of the museum experience.

IDENTIFYING DIVERSE TARGET AUDIENCES

Museums that understand their own brand will understand the character—the psychographics as well as demographics—of their donor pool. For example, many small museums rely on seasonal visitors: winter snowbirds or summer beach house crowds. It's important to realize that even though these part-time people will support the museum, their hearts and motivations may lie with their hometown institutions. Another example: upscale suburbs may seem homogenous and easily classified. Yet the turnover is great in these corporate communities with new profiles and motivations moving in constantly.

Another elusive demographic: African Americans. As a large museum in a major southeast city has discovered, church is where many African Americans hear the opinions and suggestions they trust most. Traditional museum marketing, which favors direct mail, outdoor boards, on-site events, and networking through existing members, so far has totally missed African Americans. The southeast museum is now marketing through the churches. As museums reach out to new markets—markets that are willing and able to give—they must identify and use new channels.

Age is a tricky question, at either end of the spectrum, because so many stereotypes get bandied about. Older people are likely targets because they have the erudition and money. Young parents are popular targets because they want to educate their children. Ignored in this simplistic formula are much older people and teenagers. With both groups, branding is important. Prospects who can't physically visit a building will retain loyalty to an institution when the brand is strong. Teens who are just beginning to explore cultural options want to discover their own brands; they will stay involved with museums that remember them.

Income level is another category that should be reconsidered. Many people with low incomes will dig deep into their pockets for learning they can identify with; it is a source of pride and satisfaction. People of vast resources, on the other hand, have legions of cultural institutions vying for their patronage; they may prove a very difficult target to solicit if the brand isn't relevant.

Finally, don't forget the thank-yous. Whether it's a handwritten note, a typed letter, or a gift basket, recognition is the next step in building a committed supporter.

Corporate Partnerships

Shoulder to Shoulder with Business

Involvement with businesses has always been a quiet part of museum life, from donors to sponsors. Small museums have been especially ingenious in integrating local businesses into their plans. Sometimes the lure of meaningful dollars results in flamboyant partnerships, where the scholarship of exhibitions gets buried under the surface glitter, but these exceptions hide a basic truth: museums that start to resemble Walt Disney World are not appealing partners for corporate America, which already has plenty of dazzle to draw on. Businesses are looking for the prestige that only museums can bring, and scholarly, well-curated, prestigious brands, of any size, are what business partners are seeking.

When and how to collaborate with corporate America can be examined as a business decision, but it also must be considered from a branding perspective. Will the alliance enhance the museum's mission and image, and at the same time support the corporate partner's marketing strategy? Museums need money and businesses need respectability. Museums need more people in the form of attendance and members. Business needs more people in the form of new and diverse markets. This symbiotic relationship looks so good that it's easy to forget the branding aspect: the linkup must fit comfortably with the museum's organizational culture, its personality, and its brand.

When selecting a corporate ally, keep in mind the reasons this company is interested in your museum. It may be the type of objects you collect, the reputation of your collection, your physical plant, the reputation of your curators, your location, your membership list, a new project or acquisition, or your name. All these assets must be protected in the new alliance. The solid reputation and high-mindedness that define museums are the intangible properties that corporations covet. Which is simply to say that they need you and you can afford to be picky. The caveat is to work only with corporations that share your goals. The danger is not losing your soul to business but losing your brand.

KNOW YOUR BRAND

Before you talk to any business, know your brand and be able to define it in one sentence. Every businessperson from salesperson up through CEO knows how efficiently branding oils the machinery of business, and everyone in the museum family should know the importance of brand and image. This first step in dealing with corporations denotes what you stand for and what you have to offer business partners.

This is especially true with sponsorships. Having a corporation underwrite an exhibition is a time-honored alliance. But note the true definition of a sponsor and beware of adopting just any relation; the chosen one must share your values. This shared interest must be maintained in today's high-priced sponsorships. When two logos appear on the same exhibition catalog or panel, both must reflect the spirit of the show. With so many businesses and museums pairing up, it's harder today to find a match, but wait for Mr. or Ms. Right.

If you're looking for exhibition sponsorship, those are of limited scope and duration and the timing has to fit the corporation's marketing schedule. Selecting the right exhibition at the right time can be very strategic for the corporation, so it behooves the museum to be as flexible as possible. Ongoing sponsorship usually involves operational support for the museum as a whole, rather than an individual exhibit, and here the match is with the museum's mission, rather than an individual exhibit. Don't be timid about asking for large funds; it shows you're serious and have long-range plans. Remember that the cost of sponsorship, say, $50,000 to $200,000, is small compared to an ad budget and fully deductible when it comes from a corporation's community relations budget.

A long-term sponsor relationship brings in more than money. Through their employees, shareholders, and vendors, businesses bring many new people into your circle, and new databases for membership. Good businesses contribute fresh ideas, from vastly different perspectives. Some museum diehards say that the business of business is business, and should stay that way. But smart businesspeople know a lot about history, art, science, technology, research, and display. They are valued long-term partners.

THEIR NAME VS. YOUR NAME

If your business partner's name is better known than yours, it will help you acquire awareness and raise your stature. On the other hand, you might get lost in the shuffle. If you put their logo next to yours on a brochure or newspaper ad announcing an exhibition, it will function as a seal of approval. Or it might dominate and make readers wonder whose exhibition it is. Have a corporate representative appear at your benefit and that affair will seem more glamorous. Or their trained spokesperson might speak better than your scholarly director. Be aware of these realities, which happen in any partnership, and be prepared to work them out in advance. Again, choose your teammate wisely.

Also pay attention to the corporate culture, or inner workings, of your proposed partner. The product or service might be a perfect match, but the way of doing business might prove too cautious or too aggressive. A business that's just cut back on staff might not move as adroitly as your highly adaptable staff. A company with an unadventurous board of directors might jettison your collaboration that the marketing manager initiated. A business with a hierarchy of managers and assistants might work too impersonally for your type of organization. None of these need be problems, just situations to be aware of.

As in any business venture, you must remain diligent. Ask friends and advisors about the company. Find out what other not-for-profits the company has teamed with. Visit the company Web site to learn more about their products and services and research past activity in their online press room. Send several of your staffers to the business itself—its offices or stores—to get a sense of its image and personality. In most companies, the people implementing the partnership are not the ones who brokered it, and it's permissible to ask who you'll actually be working with. Real understanding takes place when museums invite their business partners for a tour. Once they experience your product, and understand your mission, you're ready for business.

Cause-related marketing is a short-term form of corporate sponsorship that, at its simplest, agrees that a percentage of all a business's sales be contributed to the museum. In return, the company receives the right to state this fact in its advertising and other promotions. The company gets credit for generosity and takes tax write-offs, the museum enjoys additional funds and increased attendance. Both benefit from association with the other's good name. These sponsorships usually develop around a specific opportunity such as a new building, fund-raising campaign, or museum anniversary.

With business booming for product placement in TV shows and movies, there's no reason not to write a museum scene into the script. There are special marketing agencies that handle these negotiations, and although money is usually involved, it is a negotiation and worth some investigation.

Licensing is another proven business collaboration, and historic houses and restored villages have licensed their names to everything from house paint to home furnishings. Affiliating your museum's good name to appropriate products and services opens many new channels—retail stores, themed catalogs, restaurants, and interior designers, to name a few—for reaching visitors, members, donors, and other constituencies.

With sponsored prizes and awards, museums highlight their scholarly, advocacy side. Awarding monetary prizes—named for corporate sponsors—to scholars, artists, or other leaders in the field positions both museum and sponsor in a new light. The variety of categories is endless; a little brainstorming will result in awards such as best junior historian, most promising local scientist, emerging artist of the year, or leader in sustainable habitats. Of course, the corporate donor whose name is used will be selected for appropriateness to your mission. Awards to individuals always garner a lot of local publicity and there's no limit to how many people you can honor, or how often the prizes are conferred.

A corollary honor goes to the business sponsors themselves, for their contribution to historic preservation, scientific inquiry, or the arts. Don't limit your search by size. Small businesses deserve as much credit as large ones. Conversely, don't be afraid to approach one of the major leaguers.

CORPORATE TRAINING

In today's business climate, human resources departments are charged to develop talent internally, as well as to retain employees through enrichment and morale-boosting activities. The training industry has benefited for years from the insights of nonbusiness groups such as improvisational theater companies, and museums can follow suit with programs that teach needed business skills such as communication, leadership, teamwork, and problem solving. HR managers find museum educators to be extraordinarily skilled at challenging people to think creatively and imagine situations outside their own cultural parameters. Surprising though it may seem, many of the techniques used to guide school children also motivate adults. The best part of these money-making programs is that they relate so immutably to your brand.

EDUCATIONAL PROGRAMS

Compared to training programs, which can actually make money, the more traditional lectures or presentations to business groups are a softer sell. Most museums send out lecturers gratis or for a small honorarium. Yet the benefit is great for both parties. The Department of Human Resources looks on these programs as bonuses and morale boosters in times of overwork and stress. They are also looked upon as career enhancers; continuing education looks good on a resume and pushes the employee up the promotion ladder.

Outreach programs geared to businesspeople do a good job of creating awareness for, and suggesting a visit to, the museum, but the real advantage comes when the museum identity is so meaningful that affinity is born. Museums that leave an attendance sheet often sign up new members and volunteers.

An informative, entertaining lecture will be only that unless your name is attached. Then it becomes Your Museum's lecture and this is easily accomplished with a podium sign, table tents, name tags, and your logo on every slide of the presentation. Visual branding gives you ownership of the employees' enrichment program.

Workplace lectures extend beyond lecture hall and after the one-hour presentation is over, there's a residue of goodwill that you can extend to three other groups: first, the friends and families of employees; second, the professional association of human resources professionals; and third, the person in the corner office who pays for enrichment programs. To cultivate these three groups and broadcast your good name even further, prepare and use printed follow-up materials.

For attendees at the program, leave behind simple brochures or more elaborate folders with multiple pieces such as brochures, news article reprints, photographs, and information on volunteer opportunities. If there's no money for these materials, liberally hand out your business card, being sure to remember the support personnel such as the audio/visual person, or the assistant checking names at the door. Other items to stack in the lecture room include discount coupons, calendars, or tickets—all with museum logo, address, and telephone number. Also provide comment cards for participants to fill out; they're good for feedback and excellent at giving new friends a stake in the museum.

Send a thank-you letter to the HR coordinator, telling him or her how much you enjoyed the experience and, if possible, complimenting the participants' questions. Include a questionnaire (printed on letterhead) and encourage suggestions to improve the talk for next time. Follow this letter with periodic reminders of new programs.

Write a letter to the president or head of office, commending the good working relationship with the HR coordinator. Chief executives, accustomed to fund-raising solicitations, will find the thank-you note a refreshing and distinctive reminder of the fine museum in the neighborhood.

DIVERSITY PROGRAMS AND HERITAGE

Of particular interest to top management is diversity, a huge issue that museums do an extremely good job of addressing. Museum collections, by definition, are inclusive. Heritage programs exemplify the unique contributions of individual groups. Art movements and innovations, the very history of art, are progressions from one distinct group to another. And museum education programs cater to diverse groups. Museums are in a unique position to talk about diversity, to both business and community groups. And they should.

LARGE DONATIONS VS. SMALL

Subtle sponsorships and altruistic outreach programs may seem more brand-sensitive than outright solicitations, yet organizations as well as people like to give to museums with which they feel an affinity. More important, they like to be asked. Smaller donations tend to reflect more accurately the goals of the individual museum. On the other hand, it might be easier to find the proper match between your mission and that of a large corporation because they have a wide range of community organizations that strategically fit their plans. Whether soliciting large gifts or small, it's the match between giver and receiver, not just the need of the receiver, that's important. Finding the right link sometimes involves non-monetary contributions.

Although many corporate collections have pieces a museum would love to acquire, they may come prepackaged, already-curated into mini-exhibitions. A notable corporation art collection was recently disassembled and distributed among twenty-nine art institutions. This globally publicized generosity came bundled in "ways that made sense" to the donor's private curator, but not necessarily to the museums' curators.

PARTIES

Corporate functions held on museum premises are not outright gifts but their value is great; they raise the institution's profile from the moment the invitations go out. Parties, especially company affairs, receive widespread and positive awareness, and that makes brand recognition easier. Not only is the museum name and logo in the invitation, on at least one logo-tagged item in the gift bags, and behind the podium, but the museum itself is an integral part of the entire evening. To get access to the business's mailing list, either ask for it or leave well-designed response cards at the entrance.

The costs are always a concern, and they don't stop at insurance, added staff, and wear and tear. A well-publicized event could dilute your brand image and even emit the scent of elitism. A company whose corporate image doesn't reflect your core values might well want to join forces anyway, but mismatches can backfire and there's a time to say no. In negotiating the contract, retain the right to disallow signs, performances, or themes that cast you in the wrong light.

UNDERWRITTEN PARTIES

When a museum gives its own party, underwriters' financial backing will pay for a lot of impact, some of it in a higher quality event, some expressed in splashiness. Before buying the floral arrangements, make sure your image is heightened, not altered, by the exalted budget. Pay attention to everything from the tone of the party to the look of the invitation to the thrust of the speeches. Also, the underwriting of a large event usually doesn't cover the wear and tear on staff.

THE PROPOSAL TRAFFIC JAM

Once business partners have been identified, and the range of possible collaborations narrowed, prepare for a lot of traffic. Yours isn't the only cultural institution that craves funds from the prosperous businesses in town, the local foundation, or the friendly multimillionaire. Don't get your solicitation on their crowded calendars until you have a strong brand pitch. With your own brand exquisitely honed to a brief description, the main part of the pitch is directed to the donor's brand and current marketing goals, and how the two organizations interlock seamlessly. Even with a proposal of obvious mutuality, remember the other basics of good salesmanship: pick your contact and your timing as carefully as you pick your words.

Business liaisons can be initiated at any time and with small measures. You don't have to plan a major event or program. Offering artifacts from the museum as a loan to local businesses for their reception areas and conference rooms and offices is one way to start the conversation. Moving back to the museum's turf, promoting businessperson's lunches in your café offers a change of scene to neighborhood workers who might not stay or take their families on weekends. Museums without restaurants can bring in catered lunches that give a glimpse of the galleries. Brown-bag lunches, accompanied by a lecture, are a third option.

To get a foot in the door of local businesses, ask for in-kind gifts for the fair or auction. Value is secondary to the casual conversation. The sweep can include everyone from the car dealership to the gourmet shop, with special attention to providers of services. Gifts of shrub pruning or cleaning of an heirloom wedding dress are popular not just for their lower costs and novelty but for brand continuity. It's a way to create a match.

In talking to the employers, remember the employees. A once-a-year mailing of free admission tickets is an employee benefit the boss doesn't pay for. Volunteerism is another way to curry favor at every level. Management knows that service to the community shores up the economy of the area, and when a museum is thus involved in the community, the brand gains luster.

To shine your light a little farther, sign up as a stop on spouse tours during trade shows and conferences. Contact your local conference and tourism office to place your museum on their list or to help them develop a city tour for conference planners. Other organizations help museums broaden their sphere of influence. Rotary, for example, partners with cities around the globe in cultural and business exchanges. To really spread your wings, join the Business Baseball League, take off the white gloves and swing for the bleachers.

■ ■ ■

Business camaraderie is inclusive and it makes for rich partnerships. Corner office and storefront, people you've only heard of and vendors you work with daily: all are happy to shake hands with the neighborhood culture business.

TEN CHIMNEYS

FOUNDATION

MUSEUM STORE

DESIGN FOR LIVING

The museum store at Ten Chimneys, the restored Wisconsin retreat of Broadway legends Alfred Lunt and Lynne Fontanne, is a textbook example of branding. The store is named "A Design for Living," after the Noel Coward play that made their fame. Merchandise ranges from reproduction steamer trunks to glamorous perfume bottles, and pieces are tagged with cards that describe a design for living: love of theater, country living, and 1930s and 1940s sophistication. These themes guide all of the store's buying. Writing and concept by Erika Kent and the Ten Chimneys Foundation museum store team. Design by J. Scott Nolte.

10

Marketing and Graphics

The Watchdog Department

While everybody is responsible for maintaining the brand, the marketing and graphics department has the greatest opportunity to lose it. The brand look, or visible image, is so potent that when it deviates from the established, it's as good as gone. Every time a museum changes its tag line, or tries some new design formats, or varies its writing style, it feels like a different museum. On the other hand, every time a marketing piece reiterates its tag line, repeats its design format, and hews to its writing style, it feels like the old, familiar museum. No marketer can afford to keep switching its look; there isn't a big enough budget in the universe to keep customers loyal if the image keeps wandering.

A brand must pass many checkpoints to make it through the marketing and graphics department intact. Even experienced marketing experts need to watch out for brand wobbliness, for with a museum's many publics— including visitors, members, donors, sponsors, educators, the business community, the neighborhood, scholars, employees, suppliers, government, and the media—there are many different marketing materials produced. With all the different designers, writers, photographers, illustrators, and printers working on any given job, careful stewardship of the brand is essential.

Brand consistency would be easy to enforce if museums realized how much effort is saved by always using the same logo, tag line, typeface, format, and style. A more subtle, but equally important saving, is realized when the brand is used consistently. Ads can be smaller and run less often, brochures shorter, mailings less frequent and less bulky because you don't need to keep explaining who you are and what you do. Museums save money, time, and aggravation by following the amazingly efficient law of consistency: Don't change the mission. Don't change the message. Don't change the look. Don't reinvent the wheel.

THE LOOK

When art directors and designers talk about "the look" of a marketing piece, they include every visual element from the typeface to the colors. It takes a visual person to see all these details and it helps if all museum people learn how to be think visually, since looks communicate your brand as distinctly as words do. By the way, the typeface in which words are set is also a visual. To teach yourself this graphic form of communication, take a brochure in one hand and a pencil in another and work your way from top to bottom of every page; everything your pencil encounters is a visual and each influences your brand.

Now feel your letterhead stationery and make sure you haven't switched to lighter, cheaper paper. Check your business cards to see if the most recent printer captured the ink color correctly. Look at the schedule of tours on the sign at the information desk and see if the type font is your font. Thumb through the employee and volunteer handbooks to see how often the logo and other design elements are used, and whether the paper is the same quality as you hope for from your workers. Pick up a press kit and pray that the folder bears your logo, color palette, and type font. Every marketing piece, external or internal, that communicates anything about the museum must be brand conscious. Never let the reader wonder for a minute what museum he or she is looking at.

Although it's difficult for a museum to be picky about photographs (which are frequently donated), and photographers (who can be expensive to hire), they can, at the very least, be selective after the fact. Select photos that best represent the mission, that show the building, and that contain relevant props. Smiling heads are a constant in all newsletters, so try to shoot people in front of an exhibit, or holding a prop, or in front of a sign with the museum's name.

Not only printed materials adhere to The Look. Effective Web sites follow the agreed style and format, too, and the same watchdog who sniffs and nudges offline efforts should peer just as closely at online graphics.

Once a museum is fortunate enough to have an established brand look, style, and format that is used in all its marketing materials, the next step is to keep it.

IN THE KNOW

Consistent, focused brand messages require, first and forever, that the marketing and graphics department know what's happening, all over the museum. Staffers should tour the collection and special exhibitions, experience the programs of the education department, hear the goals and means of development, read the plans of the board of trustees, and understand the scholarly research that informs the museum. This is a lot of knowledge but brand marketing cannot proceed uninformed.

Conversely, every department should be aware of what the others are sending through the marketing and graphics department. Curators must see the mailers that development is mailing out. Trustees need to know what's on the cover of press kits. Sales associates in the museum store must see what the Web site is selling. And everyone, every so often, should ask the marketing folks for their opinion.

When the various departments within a museum have their own budgets and can deal directly with the marketing department, the results are predictable, with every department getting its own table tent, brochure, or label, each with a different look. Small museums might find this problem a luxury, but they have their own danger zones: small, independent contractors who don't have a history with the museum or its brand don't maintain the brand look, and don't have the clout to question a dubious branding assignment. Small museums must take time with freelance designers to explain and monitor the brand image.

SMALL BUDGETS NEED EXPANSIVE IDEAS

Budgets should never be used as an excuse to cut corners, at least not until the graphics people have a chance to reevaluate costs. The graphics department knows how to keep the brand alive, regardless of budget—but they have to know from the start what the cost limits are. After drawing up a feasible marketing budget and obtaining everyone's approval, the marketing department can cost all projects accordingly. Anything can be done on a small budget when the money and goals are openly discussed. Even when unexpected shortages dictate cuts, that needn't shortchange the brand message. This takes adaptability and creative cost-cutting, but responsible marketing and graphics professionals do it all the time. Branding is not a job for the fragile and will always involve tough negotiations.

A corollary to sudden cuts is a surprise gift of money, or worse, pro bono services. This is not license to splurge, but to watch brand specifications even more rigorously. For instance, just because you can suddenly afford a four-color brochure doesn't mean you should. It changes your brand image if the brand palette has heretofore been earth tones used in two-color pieces. A flashy piece gets attention, but if it is inconsistent with prior pieces it could confuse the message. And just because designers offer to do a piece gratis does not give them free rein with the brand personality.

Budgets face the worst dangers when museums try to reach all their audiences separately, when each department wants its own material. That's where brands meet their Waterloos, too. Just because museums communicate to visitors and members and donors and educators and the community is no reason to customize the communications. These groups overlap and everyone must see the same message. An invitation to a gala might be seen by a teacher; a school tour guide proposal might land on an editor's desk.

Considering the range of materials a museum produces, maintaining consistent brand identity across the board is a huge job that relies on one mantra, repeated as often as necessary: "Is this piece on brand?" Alertness to slipping off message is a start. It's highly recommended that one person in the marketing department be charged with supervising brand continuity and signing off on all marketing pieces.

BRANDING VS. CREATIVITY

Creativity, ironically, is one of branding's subtlest enemies. Museums honor original thinking, but while scholarship must be creative and education programs utilize creativity, rampant creativity in marketing materials can sabotage solid branding. Nothing corrodes a brand faster than irresponsible bursts of creation that veer from the established brand look. The brand is always simple and clear; it is itself creative because it represents your unique museum. It needs no fancy dress and does not flaunt new conceits with every new marketing piece. The only way to judge the creativity of a marketing piece—brochure, invitation, press kit, or ad—is by the way it enhances the brand. The marketing and graphics people implement the brand best when they are alerted early in the planning stages of a project and can hear firsthand the rationale behind it.

TAG LINE—THE LITTLE WORDS THAT SUM UP YOUR MISSION

If all branded marketing materials start with a look, they end with a tag line. The tag line is the short phrase that appears below or beside a logo, a wrap-up to the message. The tag line defines what your institution stands for. It appears on ads, brochures, Web sites, radio commercials, letterhead, uniforms, signage, menus, merchandise tags, press releases, interviews, invoices, and other printed and spoken communications.

A tag line ties your multifaceted marketing efforts into a coherent whole. The tag line is efficient, because each individual piece is seen as a continuation of the main message. The tag line is a memorable, shorthand expression that extols your museum wherever it is seen. A small budget stretches much farther with the same tag line on every piece.

A few rules pertain to tag lines, the first being: keep the same tag line and keep it to one. Despite the fun and ease of cranking out lots of clever slogans, after the brainstorming sessions end, just one line must emerge. It's inclusive and effective to open up the tag line process, inviting the suggestions of staff and volunteers, and testing one line against others. This puts thoughts on core values on the table, where all concerned parties can debate them. It may be the only time when everyone in the museum has a chance to discuss brand and mission, and come together with a common goal. The danger is compromising a clear-cut branding position by flattering everyone and combining several tag lines. However enticing multiple tag lines may be, they split your personality into pieces. Choosing just one is staggeringly difficult, but stick with it and then band together to use it. It's your signature.

The need for a tag line becomes evident at the beginning of a capital campaign, when strangers want to know who you are and why you're more deserving than other institutions. Going through the tag line process provides the concise answer. Foundations also want to know your unique place in their deliberations and grant writing begins with a point-of-view that should be as clear as a tag line. The tag line is an inexhaustible ally. When a prospective donor, or employee, or editor says, "Tell me about your museum," all you need say is the tag line.

After completing the time-consuming but relatively inexpensive job of creating a tag line, you can begin the logo development, which can be costly. This task is best given to experienced designers who know how to create an identity program usable on all materials. It's not just a matter of creating a unique marque, but of finding one that will reproduce on all materials, in all sizes, and in black and white as well as color. It must look as good on a glossy press kit as it does on a merchandise label or visitor tag. Whether seen on a wall label, podium, or board minutes, it must be seen as the embodiment of the museum. The typeface that carries the tag line must work with the logo and be both distinctive and readable. And the logo and tag line entity must travel well, whether by electronic file, photocopy, or fax.

The process of selecting a designer is key. Interview several, get recommendations from other clients, and make sure the candidates have experience working with not-for-profits. Make sure the designer understands your brand and is willing to live with it over a period of time. Most logos take longer than expected to complete and designers end up making less money than they thought. You don't want them to feel frustrated. Realize also that designers like to show logos in their portfolios and might want to get overly design-y (and under-performing) with yours.

A successful logo, and logo designer, will go through many iterations. After the initial concept has been selected, there are choices of style, period, and technique. The same image can be modern, colonial, global, or grunge. A logo created with a paintbrush look will convey a different identity than one that looks chiseled, and computer software has made the variables of design limitless, with very little effort. Good graphics professionals, by nature and training, look at simple ideas from dozens of perspectives. They try and discard, and try again.

At any stage of the tag line and logo process, focus groups are a good idea. Internal groups, chosen from administration, curators, board members, employees, volunteers, and even visitors, cost little and provide valuable insights on the effectiveness of the communication.

The months of effort spent on developing a logo cannot be calculated in dollars and branding soldiers don't even try. Identity is not a line item, one museum marketing director declared. It can't be separated from the total museum.

Identity is a major part of the museum director's job. Although he or she may speak about the collection, exhibitions, or budget needs, mainly they are conveying identity. One director said, "My responsibility as director is branding."

EVERY SURFACE IS A MARKETING TOOL

With a good logo and tag line, and a history of consistent marketing pieces, museums can go forward confidently and find new opportunities for displaying the brand. When the typeface is used accurately, and the palette of colors is established and adhered to, the look, logo, and tag line are ready to go on all materials seen by the public. This includes all the usual marketing pieces, plus overlooked surfaces such as exhibit labels, every page of the Web site, invoices, store merchandise tags, café menus, all educational material (even those handed out to grammar school students, which are seen by their teachers and parents), audio tour wands, employee manuals, the printed agenda at board meetings, and the podium at lectures.

Because business cards are such a frequently seen surface, they deserve special graphic attention. Not only should they deliver the identity of the museum, but its personality. Many companies now state their mission on the back of the cards.

When cosponsoring events with corporations, local businesses, or other not-for-profit institutions, museums can negotiate the size and placement of their logo. Neither partner should be overshadowed by the other. At all events, museum people should wear name tags with the logo to remind event and meeting attendees that it's a museum event they're attending and a museum friend with whom they're sharing the experience. This applies to volunteer meetings, garden walks, and small programs, as well as large public events or benefits.

Keep a watchdog's eye on large visual areas, as well as the small ones. For example, invite a visual person to check out the lobby; that is, after all, the visitor's first and last impression of the museum. When your meeting rooms are used by business or community groups, identify them boldly. This could be wall signage, with logo, or notepads and pencils with logo. At the very least, set out a stack of brochures large enough to invite taking. If you have bought space in kiosks in airports, malls, convention centers, or other heavily trafficked area, use the logo double strength. It will be competing with dozens of other visuals for the attention of an easily distracted audience.

There's one surface that also sees a lot of traffic, and is unequaled in branding power: the museum store shopping bags. It should be designed with panache and supplied with even the smallest purchase. This is potent word-of-mouth advertising that buzzes for a long time, over a long distance.

Newspaper ads are a potential identity problem because there's so much to say about the exhibition itself, and newspaper space is so costly that the name of the museum gets squeezed in whatever space is left. Be sure to save plenty of room in the ad for the logo and tag line; don't let the objects overwhelm the museum itself. For significant cost efficiency, college newspapers merit investigation; they're inexpensive and reach an attractive target.

E-mail announcements also are space challenged and require deft writing. The subject area should always use the same wording, preferably the name of the museum and one or two other words, such as "News from the Smith Zoo: Baby Panda," or "This Month at the Jones House: Winter Parlor Games."

As for the marketing vehicles that use sound, here is where the tag line carries the full weight of your identification. Make sure broadcast journalists and interviewers have the tag line as well as the name of the museum. If they use the tag line, that's publicity plus, and at the very least they have a concise articulation of your mission. Don't squander the good fortune of a television interview. Put a large sign with the name of your museum behind your spokesperson. The station may edit out your good lines, but they can't edit out the sign. Pay attention also to the announcer voice on radio commercials and recorded messages so that it sounds like the personality of the museum.

11

Museum Store

Extension of Education

Museum stores have practiced good branding longer than any other part of the museum. In their role of educational extensions, those emporiums, some only counters, dramatically contribute to the image of, and loyalty to, the entire museum. Good branding at retail includes the merchandise itself, packaging, signage, staff attitude, and the mystique of the retail space.

Americans love to shop and love ownership, and this bodes well for a museum. Visitors who have purchased a *souvenir*—which is, of course, a memory—remember exhibits better, recall more fondly their experience, and spread the word more sincerely to friends. With one little cash register receipt you have converted a visitor to a loyalist.

MEMORY MERCHANDISE

Stocking items that reflect the collection or exhibitions sounds simple but, like everything else in branding, takes fastidious attention. It's easy to be swayed by a sure-selling toy, book, or piece of jewelry. However, just as merchandisers demand a price point, museum merchants demand relevance. It takes some talking: with vendors to get the right items and enlist their help for suggestions, with local artisans to create special items, and with curators to understand what's in an exhibition that store merchandise must relate to.

Covering all prices ranges is important; stores want to send their shoppers home with something. But visitors like upscale merchandise, too, because it reinforces the quality of the exhibits and enhances the value of the visit. Uncommon items, even if unfamiliar to the market, give shoppers new ideas, which are a good way to engender loyalty—the reason why people come to museums in the first place. Visitors expect above-average merchandise in the store and they'll remember the museum better because of it.

Locally made products add to your regional identity. The Cedar Rapids (Iowa) Museum of Art offers a stunning selection of work by local artisans that reinforces its image. The Ute Indian Museum sells, in addition to Native American–made jewelry and pottery, bottled water from a spring on the nearby Northern Ute Tribal reservation. Nu-Pah Spring Water, from the same under-the-mountain source that provided water for traditional ceremonies, must rank near the top of brilliant museum store relevance.

Relevance comes in many containers, and the CD reflects a museum's identity in both sound and image. Some museums assemble their own collection of songs, but it's just as effective to offer songs or sounds that might have been played in a historic home, or in the era covered by the museum, or in the sounds of a garden. At The Frick Collection in New York City, a small sign announces, "Mr. Frick's Favorites," music played on an Aeolian pipe organ built on the staircase landing of his Fifth Avenue mansion. This makes for very effective branding at the point of sale, especially when the CD case reproduces artwork from the house.

LOGO RESTRAINT

Details count. Logos should be used with caution and not plunked down on any mug or bookmark. In most cases, it will do no more harm than to associate a museum's name with a cliché item. There might be situations where a generic product runs counter to the brand, as a coffee mug might if the museum dates from tea-party colonial times. Dull items are, of course, to be avoided, or at least balanced by imaginative ones.

Attention should be paid to the quality of materials used in the fabrication of items such as pottery or quilts; they may look less than authentic. And it pays to question the "ingredients" of a product. A Victorian music box playing "Lara's Theme" would be as tasteless and wrong as a nineteenth-century recipe book calling for canned mushroom soup. Appropriate articles need not be expensive and authenticity can be reasonably priced, but while cost is negotiable, the reflection on museum image is not.

Some visitors shop for their own use, some for their family back home, and some for gifts. Many are men and, more and more, quite a few are locals who bypass the museum altogether. Each is buying a piece of the museum, however, and will read its identity every time the item is used. The selection will range from practical to luxurious, fun to educational, and all must be in sync with the museum's mission. This is especially important because there are other markets for the store, beyond the visitor or shopper, people whose support must be nurtured. These include volunteers, members and donors, corporate sponsors, local businesses, government officials, and the media. The store is a way to give a tangible part of you, an actual mnemonic device, to these stakeholders.

Volunteers, members, and donors should be encouraged to use the store for their own personal gift lists, just as volunteer appreciation awards should be store-bought. Gifts of store merchandise to corporate sponsors give these worthies a quick, tangible perspective on the museum. And small items in press kits add personality that help the media shape their stories. Thinking of the store as a marketing tool, as well as a marketplace, it makes sense to give the store street presence with appropriate signage.

BOOKS AND BRAND

Books, beloved though they are, present a branding problem because they're generic. Unless books are written specifically about your museum, or have been authored by people closely associated with it, they divert attention from the mission. To benefit from the satisfaction and pride that adheres to a book purchase, short curator-written book reviews, placed around the shelves, will connect them with the museum. The museum can "own" the book by pasting a bookplate on the inside cover with the logo and the words: "A gift of knowledge from the [name of museum]." Less permanent, but equally effective, is a well-designed bookmark with the same message.

Tags and bags are important components of a museum store and make for smart branding investments. A tag with logo immediately communicates a relationship between the merchandise and the mission of the museum. If time and staff allow, written comments on the tags, as done by antique stores, make the connection clear. Ten Chimneys, the restored

Wisconsin retreat of actors Alfred Lunt and Lynne Fontanne, has perfectly joined its store to its mission. The store name is Design for Living, not only one of the Lunts' signature plays, but their philosophy. The store's label lists the criteria used in selecting merchandise; they must embody "gracious entertaining, love of theatre, country living, 1930s and 1940s sophistication," the personality that informs the museum itself.

Speaking of store names, "Museum Store" seems to be the default name. However, this is generic. "Crossroads Trading Company," the Caldwell Zoo (Tyler, Texas) store that features African motif items, not only distinguishes this zoo from all others, it also positions the store as an extension of the museum's educational mission. The Tienda, at the Mexican Fine Arts Center Museum in Chicago, has the appearance of a cultural marketplace and the name confirms it. As an extension of the museum that extends far beyond its wall, shopping bags with your logo and colors are essential. This is the cheapest advertising available, because everyone who leaves with a purchase is a mobile billboard. Bags get used long after the visit, so this advertising has frequency as well as reach. More important, they make the purchaser feel proud, a member of a special club, carried like a badge of honor. A visitor once said, "When I carry a shopping bag from a museum, I feel like it's enhancing my brand image."

Top sellers in most museums stores are postcards, and even these commodity items can be branded. The Courtauld Institute of Art in London puts its logo, screened back to a light image, across the entire back of its postcards. Immediately, just another picture has become the Courtauld's message.

THE RETAIL SPACE

The store is the one space in a museum where visitors feel free to talk out loud, where they can relax, reflect, and share reactions to the museum. Big museums have restaurants, lobbies, and hallways where this familiarization can begin. Small museums always have the gift counter, an area that should be as welcoming as size and budget allow.

INTERIOR DÉCOR

As a continuation of the interpretation in exhibition spaces, the interior of the store displays merchandise for easy studying. That means easy to see tabletops and cases, and a chair or two to revive the spirit before shopping resumes. Stores short of shelf space can intersperse books and objects: the Utah Museum of Natural History places reproduction pottery near books on the subject, and uses geodes for bookends. Some dramatization is allowable in stores that, after all, are supposed to continue the gallery experience, and music would be a start. Appropriate music underscores mission and brand, much as it does in commercial establishments and more and more museum exhibitions, and is readily available in any genre. For special exhibitions, borrow from department stores and bring in a live musician.

Aromas can be pulled out of obscurity to do motivational duty. Spiced cider and baked goods aren't only for holiday events in house museums. Smell is a powerful reminder of experiences, whether it hints at an actual exhibit or merely enhances the ambience of the store.

Living museums have demonstrated how successfully visitors enter into the spirit of the museum when they are greeted throughout by costumed interpreters. Without changing the store's format, adding a hat or apron instantly suggests an era, a region, or a culture, and serves as a powerful prop to enhance the store's ambiance and meaning.

Though the retail space extends the museum, in one sense it improves on it: touch. Unlike the no-touch galleries, in the store, everything for sale is for touch. Flaunt this fact and put visitors in closer touch with the brand.

PREVIEW AND REVIEW

A store situated within sight of the exhibits will remind visitors of the connection between the two. If they visit the store at the beginning of the visit—and many do just that to get their bearings—they'll be prepped to better appreciate what lies ahead. If they stop at the end of their visit it will serve as a summary of what's been seen. Some managers, perhaps in the belief that mercantilism is too commercial, bury their stores in far corners or basements. This is unfortunate. Even if no transaction takes place, the store sends visitors away better educated and satisfied. As proof of the importance of the store, in most museums one can shop without paying entrance fees. Because many shoppers believe their purchases are keeping the museum solvent, it behooves staffers to keep the store brisk, vigorous, and successful looking. If the store sells apparel and accessories, a full-length mirror would gratify shoppers immensely.

MUSEUM STORE PERSONNEL

Quietly, and behind the scenes, sales assistants are your frontline branding agents, representing your brand on every purchase. In fact, in small museums, they are the only information desk. If they are good salespeople, and they should be well trained, they will be knowledgeable about the merchandise, able to explain the item much as a wall label does. In their conversations with the customers they can relate an item to the museum's mission. After docents put your mission into the mind of the visitor, store staffers put it in their hands.

MARKET RESEARCH FROM THE SALES FLOOR

The people who work in the stores also provide insightful market research, since they're the ones who interact daily with the customer. What is heard and observed is quality intelligence for curators, docents, directors, and trustees. People who sell relate to the customer, ask thoughtful questions, and get revealing answers. Imagine the insights one could learn by asking the question a sales assistant once posed to a purchaser: "And what memory of the museum are you taking home with you today?"

You don't need expensive, time-consuming, professional research to obtain information. Start by simply urging your staff to talk to customers and listen carefully. As part of store training, include a special seminar in research gathering. Give your staff a checklist of behaviors to watch for and encourage them to jot down comments. Bring them together to compare notes, and invite a few people from the curatorial staff and the education department to sit in. Some observations might include length of time in the store, length of time with any one item, first area or item visitors head for, books opened, and items shown to companions.

The Museumbuttik at the Vesterheim Norwegian-American Museum themes tightly around all things Norwegian, with lots of nisse (gnomes), Norwegian imports such as sweaters and glassware, books published in Norwegian, and baking equipment for Norwegian recipes. Generic pioneer or rural mementos don't make the cut. Shop visitors want to have something Norwegian in their homes, and other nationalities come to the store with the same intent, and the museum has done its homework on consumer preferences. To make sure that all shoppers, Norwegian-centric or not, understand the ware, signage describes the items and recipe cards for authentic dishes are displayed next to the cookware.

Store personnel, who are experienced, trained, and paid, watch what sells and remove from the list any generic immigrant era items. Clerks all have a specialty area that they maintain, that they can speak knowledgably about to customers. Every purchaser leaves the store carrying publicity for the store. Generic shopping bags are branded with museum logo stickers, the same stickers that are affixed to lapels at the entrance. The museum likes the stick-ons because people forget to remove them and become walking billboards around town. An equally important contributor to the museum, albeit a for-profit one, is the Hanverk Store, which supplies materials for the rosemaling craft classes taught above the shop.

■ ■ ■

Small counter or large emporium, museum stores make the experience ownable, and ownership is good for remembering a brand. Some shoppers will buy, and some will look, but all will leave the store with an enhanced memory of the museum.

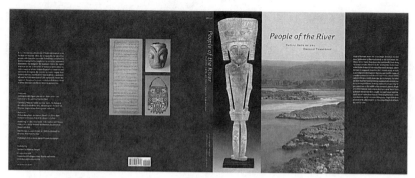

Catalogs reinforce the museum's message on the shelf, online, in the hands, and for years afterward in the home. As with "People of the River: Native Arts of the Oregon Territory" catalog, which documents an exhibition closely tied to the identity and mission of the Portland Art Museum, catalogs are souvenirs in the truest sense of the word: they are memories. Courtesy of Portland Art Museum.

12

Branding Museum Web Sites

New Media, Old Truths

The Web has become a major marketing tool, far surpassing its original use as a convenient medium for posting snapshots of the collection, museum hours, and a directional map. As museum Web sites expand to describing programs, selling merchandise, soliciting memberships, and enticing volunteers, they run the risk of diluting their identity in the wash of information. And make no mistake, at every touchpoint with the consumer, museums must reinforce their distinctive identity to instill loyalty. That's where branding comes in. The Web has progressed technologically and creatively to a branding tool par excellence. It provides the targeting and product information, and that breeds constancy.

STUDENTS TO SENATORS, MANY AUDIENCES VISIT THE WEB

There are many people whose attentions museums crave: visitors, members, donors, artists, scholars, staff, civic leaders, and governments, to name a few. And one of the places they all come face to face with the museum is the Web site. One of the more remarkable benefits of the Web is its ability, on one screen, to reach so many audiences with so much information. It's an opportunity not to be taken lightly.

With the click on a link, any museum, of any size, can use its site to discuss research projects or even conduct research, present its case to state legislatures, honor artists with biographical material, provide lesson ideas to schoolteachers, and provide background information for the media.

89

A Web site is much like any other marketing vehicle and, like a magazine ad, direct mail piece, or lobby sign, it must reflect the museum's image. It must use the same graphic elements, talk with the same tone of voice, and consistently communicate the same message. When a Web site conveys that distinctive persona, it has an unsurpassed opportunity to strengthen allegiances.

Many people are, or should be, involved in the architecture and content of the museum's Web site, so it's an opportunity for putting everyone's thoughts out on the table. It may be one of the few places that curator and educator, fund-raiser and marketer, trustee and staff can speak with one voice.

That single personality, that clear identity, is the result of practiced consistency.

CONSISTENCY OF COLOR, IMAGES, AND COPY

Effective Web sites, like all marketing media, utilize consistent images and copy to communicate their brand. The Andy Warhol Museum Web site greets the visitor with a photo of the famed artist, followed by page after page of an iconic illustrated portrait, each succeeding page, like his serial art works, in a different Warholian color. The Metropolitan Museum of Art uses a consistent palette of half a dozen subtle designer colors and the identical layout on every single page. The good news about consistency is it doesn't cost a lot of money. Any museum, of any size, can command it.

The first act of consistency is to place the museum logo on every page. As visitors move through the site, it's important for them to know where they are; if the site is interactive at all, a few clicks can lead the visitor down many a new path. This identity is even more useful when a visitor prints out a tour schedule or driving instructions. The plus benefit here is that printouts stay on desks, or get passed along, for months.

If a site has a link to a ZooCam, or order form, or survey, the logo goes along. And the logo finds a place for itself even on text-heavy, all-business pages like the News Room press release page, or Board of Trustee page. Visitors who foray deep into a site are seriously interested in getting together, and they would miss something if they couldn't immediately see its identification.

Although there is always room on the page for the logo, space is limited and not everything can squeeze on. Conflicting logos need to be scrutinized. Museums that defray the costs of expensive exhibitions by putting corporate identities on their home page run the risk of being overwhelmed by the well-known, colorful corporate look. It's allowable to negotiate for size and placement of the museum's logo.

Another trap is the people photo. Science museums, in particular, show people interacting with their exhibits. In brochures or press releases, this is de rigueur. On the small computer screen, if you show people, they frequently overshadow the gila monster or gyroscope, and that's what identifies the museum. Art museums never even get near that pitfall. Art needs no audience in the photo to bring it to life. Museums are well advised to focus on the artifact and use the magic of digital technology to animate them.

Children's museums also may yield to the temptation to tell too much on one page. It's so easy to put interactive games, questions, and other learning exercises online, that the fun obscures the identity of the museum. After a few too many animated diagrams, irresistible stories, and easy links to more knowledge pages, the viewer might well wonder if this is simply a virtual museum. Certainly, the brand is lost among the stimulation. The site is never a replacement for the museum; it's one manifestation of the brand.

COMPLEX BUT NAVIGABLE

One of the hallmarks of a good museum site is its cohesive variety. The visitor should be able to wander at will, as if through multiple galleries, without getting lost. This requires a wayfinding system of consistent page layouts, readable type fonts, and logical links. Even small Web sites should hire some objective surfers to vet the navigability of the site.

TONE OF VOICE

Just as movies have a tone of voice, so does a Web site. It comes from the attitude of the site as much as from the copy. Writers with an unswerving narrative style should be hired to write the site, to lead visitors through it. Tell a well-woven story and the world sits at your feet, waiting for the next word, and pledging unwavering attention. A good brand is one with a consistent story.

To keep visitors' fingers on the mouse, clicking through the site, Web architects use sticky features. These are pages such as the flower of the day, this day in American history, and all the repeatable interactivities that induce visitors to visit again and again. Keeping visitors in regular touch with the brand augments loyalty, so dreaming up sticky features is as important as it is fun. Consider posting letters from visitors, children's drawings (names optional for security), voting for this month's favorite painting, or downloading sound effects. Digital technology makes changing pages easy, and it is technology that should be used often.

But again, the clutter warning. It's tempting with electronic media to go eclectic, to abuse the enter-at-any-point structure. However, Web design functions best when it's not freewheeling, but clear-headed and orderly, when the pages are clean and crisp, and the text is short and legible. Web site research shows that museum visitors like the availability of additional information on demand. They respect the museum for providing extra knowledge. But their enthusiasm is based on easy clicking for more; they won't dig through thickets of type and visuals.

The global nature of museums' constituencies speaks in favor of Web site coherence. A fair percentage of Web users don't speak English, so visuals assume major importance. International visitors, whether tourists, scholars, artists, donors, or lenders, all need to understand a museum's brand distinctiveness very clearly.

Purposeful Web sites never forget what they're marketing. Museums may be selling culture, information, and ideas, but selling they are, and their online audience is a busy one. A clear message is required.

DESIGNING A WEB SITE, STEP BY STEP

The technology is so vast and its applications so approachable, that Web design can be daunting if you don't follow some fundamentals.

The foundation step is to interview several Web design teams and choose the one that you can work with. The word "team" is significant, because good Web sites are developed by writers, art directors, "architects" who know where to place drop-down menus and when to use mouse-overs, and techies who do the actual programming. Experienced Web designers will not necessarily be slick or over-packaged. Rather, they will be patient and extremely articulate. If they can't describe every term and technique they use, don't bring them back for a second interview. Good Web designers rely on the client for in-depth knowledge of your museum and its goals. Part of your selection process is how well they listen to you, and whether they ask good questions.

Designers always look to each other for inspiration and you should study other museum sites for features that you admire, or wouldn't want to emulate. As you do your own surfing, be aware of all Web sites and note down features that you like. The technology is available to everyone and can be adapted to your museum's brand and image.

After looking around, you might have a better idea of whether you want to update an existing Web site or start from scratch. Have a rough outline of the content to discuss with the Web design candidates. Inventory your photographs so you know what visuals are already available. Gather the brochures and mailings you've produced to get a sense of branding themes that should be adapted to the site. Often a patch job is more difficult to accomplish than a total makeover.

WEB DEVELOPER

Get a clear description in writing of what the Web developers include in their job. This could cover finding the service provider, designing the site and number of revisions, testing the site from many different computers, and returning months later to update the site. Find out if they charge by the job or the hour, or a combination of the two. If you update the site yourself, will they train you? Be sure the programs they use are transferable to any other developer you may subsequently retain.

Now that you have a working team you can begin to create a strongly branded Web site. If you update an existing site, be prepared to cut objectively and sweep away any elements that conflict with the brand. There will be at least one element among type fonts or images that reflects the museum's personality, and that is the element you build on.

Design your home page not for flashiness, but for instant identification; that's the first view of your brand. If you're an art museum, it makes sense to display paintings or sculpture on the home page. You're lucky, because art is, by definition, graphic and visual, and it immediately identifies your institution. With so many exhibits to choose from, it's wise to conduct an informal focus group to select the most effective and popular. If you're a science or natural history museum, limit your images to only two or three and opt for images that are bold, not complex, and easily identifiable. A scientist might think that a chart of the human genome communicates clearly, but conduct a little research to see if potential visitors might agree. Let the geologist and zoologist go head to head over geodes vs. butterflies, and then gather a group to help pinpoint the best visuals. If you're a history museum, the same guidelines apply, and you, too, will have to research the relative merits of one era or several, whole houses or furnishings, documents and/or artifacts. Invite people from different departments to the home page meeting to understand what best portrays your museum to the public. Remember that your image is more than a sum of its collection, and that you have the rest of the Web site to expand into detail.

By now, museum branders know to put the logo on every page of the site, and it pays to remind the designers up front so they'll design a template that leaves plenty of space for it, regardless of the content of each page. Museums that have used favorite illustrations or graphic devices in their materials, or several different logos, may disagree on which one to use. It's tempting to combine them, and the possible variations always heat up discussion. This is one debate that can't be avoided, and when the logo situation is resolved, everyone will come away with a much clearer image of the museum.

SIGNATURE ILLUSTRATION

The logo is one way to sign each page; a signature illustration is another. This visual signature is usually a simple illustration, or photo silhouette, and it identifies your type of museum symbolically. It could be a sculpture, historical artifact, object from nature, scientific instrument, children's toy, or industrial mechanism. The Adirondack Museum utilizes a scenic banner across the top of each page, coupled with a line illustration of a man portaging a canoe.

Single-mindedness on the logo and signature illustration will help contain the cascade of graphic elements like icons, ideographs, colored panels, and frames. Again, with many pages to work with, it's fun to sprinkle all these elements around. But not all of them! It's confusing to have too many design elements in a space that also contains plentiful information and ample visuals, not to mention a lot of type.

Type should be handled with all the same sensitivity as in brochures, and then some. Type can break up on a computer screen, and its color will vary from unit to unit. Legibility is as important as consistency, but there should be some clear distinctions. Make sure your logo is immediately readable, and different from the text font. Legible text is written in another type font. Just as your logo always is reproduced in one typeface, so your text should have a consistent look. It contributes to the overall color and emotion of a page and subconsciously identifies your museum as precisely as your logo does. Color is another identifier, and should be used as consistently as type and layout. Too much color can also confuse or distort your image. Best to select a palette of complementary hues and, of course, stay with it. A good designer understands the use of color, especially as it translates to many different computer screens.

Despite the infinite size of the Web, your surface area is only about 150 square inches, and if it's cluttered visitors will have trouble discerning your image or, worse, think your image is a scatterbrained one. Don't try to put the whole museum into the Web site. Science museums sometimes make the mistake of trying to say and show too much, and their sites come off looking frantic and whimsical, not necessarily the impression science museums want to convey.

NARRATIVE VOICE

The Web is such a visual medium that it's easy to overlook the writing. If you think of the Web site as an unfolding narrative, it will be easier to find your voice and speak consistently. This is a function of good writing and the same rules that apply to writing a brochure or catalog apply to the Web site. The tone of voice might be serious or folksy, formal or casual. One narrative style is text-heavy, with a lot of information explaining everything from exhibits to store merchandise. Another kind of narrative relies on visuals telling the story, with the aid of brief caption-like copy. The personality of the museum will help determine your voice.

Personality is easy to lose, especially in a photograph where real persons capture all the attention. Hiring an architectural or advertising photographer will put the focus back on the museum. Professionals know how to frame and light an object so it communicates the message you want to convey. There's nothing more uncommunicative than a photograph that is busy, small, or without contrast. Archival photographs can be all of the above and must be carefully selected.

What started out as an artist's medium has become more like a filmmaker's, and it's time to consider the use of sound—voice, music, or sound effect—to reinforce the identity. The sense of hearing, as much as the sense of sight, is basic to human understanding, and aids in identity of everything from an approaching car to your museum. The possibilities are endless, and a task force from various departments of the museum could draw up an actionable list of ideas. Think about period songs, actors reading letters from historic figures or artists, natural sounds like rain or a lion's roar, "scientific" sound effects, crowd sounds like applause or cheering, and archival blurbs from movies and videotapes.

ALWAYS RETURN HOME

Regardless of all the memorable art, writing, and special effects available to the Web designers, most museums will be able to handle only a few pages at first. That's fine, because the charm of the Web is the ease of adding on. When this happens, just remember to put a link to the home page on every page, so the visitor doesn't forget the institution's main message. The more rich and complex your site, the more opportunity for a visitor to literally wander away from home. Even with assiduous branding on every page, with logos and layout consistency, it's easy to get lost in the content. With this in mind, think twice about linking to other Web sites. One problem in this inclusive approach is dilution of one's own brand message. Sometimes it's impossible to return to the museum site, and when a link is a one-way street it will halt a visitor's virtual visit before the brand has time to sink in. Be cooperative and collegial, but negotiate for links back to your home page.

The goal, of course, is to keep visitors immersed in the brand as long as possible. On the other hand, the real museum should never be far away, and printable pages make that possible. For example, put a print icon on a calendar of events, or the directional map, or an artifact. Wherever appropriate, include a link to a real person's e-mail address and the assurance that the real person will promptly respond.

Use interactivity not just to titillate but to engage viewers and relate their interests with the content of the museum. Some sites contain so many interactive games that the real museum fades away. The Fort Morgan (Colorado) Museum puts interactivity to branding purpose, with a masterfully simple genealogy page (just one simple scroll-down page!) on which the visitor can submit genealogy research questions and, for a small fee, get individualized answers.

BUILDING A DATABASE

Similar creativity can be applied to building a database. Interactivity assures that every time a visitor orders from the online store, completes a pledge card, signs up for a program, or asks for information, a name is added. Look for other meaningful, interesting ways to engage visitors and acquire their names (with opt-in choices, of course). With so much research conducted online, surveys and questionnaires are appropriate ways to connect with your publics.

And while collecting visitors' names, scoop up their friends with "send to a friend" devices. Postcards with images from the collection can be sent free by e-mail to any address the viewer provides. Coupons for "one friend free" are another smart use of basic electronic technology. The promise of a visit with a companion is enough to convert a virtual Web visitor to an actual one. Both interactive features recognize that sharing the experience with a friend enhances the memories and builds loyalty.

Basic or full bells and whistles, all Web sites function better when paired with a follow-up e-mail program. These are sent to any names the Web site harvests. Keep virtual visitors informed and involved with your brand by notifying them of new exhibitions, listing the month's calendar of events, or printing the next issue of the newsletter. Look for reasons to stay in regular contact with site visitors. If the online store promotes a new store item each month, it's just the kind of sticky feature that can be communicated in an e-mail and another way to keep the image in front of the public.

The infinite possibilities of a Web site are reminders of the many constituents a museum serves. One group to remember often is the media, who should be welcomed to a well-run press room page. Help journalists write a good story and they'll help your brand get mentioned. One way to help is to offer the services of experts who they can interview further.

Journalists, both print and broadcast, keep "expert lists" that they count on to fill out a story and give it credibility. Get on the list, and then respond immediately to requests for quotes or background information. You could send out press releases listing all the areas in which you have expert knowledge, but it's easier to post it on the Web site where a newsperson can verify your credentials and get a sense of your image.

THE STEPS TO A GOOD WEB SITE NEVER STOP

Updating your site is always the next step. The brilliance of the Web is its instant flexibility, the ease with which technology can update information, change visuals, and add new pages. The Web enables you to be utterly in tune with your community, to distinguish yourself by being sensitive to seasonal, economic, and social issues. To keep your Web site robust, develop a system for regularly reviewing it. A rotating committee of staffers from different departments might surf it every few months, checking for both essential changes and more subtle ones that will communicate to your world your unique significance for them.

Adirondack Museum sprawls over thirty-two acres and consists of exhibits, programs, and family recreation activities. Its Web site also expands over considerable territory and all of it is charmingly related. In the section that talks about Adirondacks summer camps of yore, letters from former campers evoke wonderful memories any reader can relate to. It's also a wonderful feature for bringing people into the site to find their name. To further engage the visitor, a sound track plays kids singing camp songs. And on every page the visitor encounters photographs showing autumnal mountains, rowboats on the lake, and wooded walks that turn this site into a storybook, quite a feat for such a large and many-layered site.

One of the best-branded sites on the World Wide Web belongs to the State Hermitage Museum, St. Petersburg, Russia. Every page is headed with a glorious four-color banner that proclaims the art to be found within. It is photographed and cropped expertly to highlight the beauty of the artwork. More significantly, to the side of the banner is a small, one-color, almost old-looking photograph of the museum building itself. Together the two images communicate the grandeur of the place and its place in history, a powerful branding message that appears on every Web page. As national borders lower, allegiance will come from all over the world, and the Web will facilitate the journey.

The Golden Shopping Cart

How Museums' Online Stores Add Luster to Their Brand

They're small and flat with only two wheels, but a touch of the finger to the shopping cart icon is all it takes to propel eager shoppers toward online checkout counters. So overwhelmingly attractive are online treasures, in fact, that they threaten to blur the brand image of museums. The online store conveys a museum's brand as distinctly as do its exhibitions, edifice, and events. It may engender even more loyalty, thanks to the exuberance of the unfettered shopper.

Time spent at the online store is no trivial matter. Popular as museums are, shopping is still the number one tourist activity. And now the virtual museum store is becoming a popular destination in its own right. Online stores must remember that shopping cart purchases are reflections on the museum and, one hopes, memories of the museum experience. Digital museum stores confront special obstacles in communicating image. Whereas brick-and-mortar stores are contiguous spaces within the museum, attached physically and visually to the museum beyond, online stores are just a click away from a potpourri of enticements, not all of them belonging to the museum. It's easy to lose sight of the main message.

The danger of an online store veering too far off brand could damage the image in donors' eyes as well. Some administrators already worry that major philanthropists might shy away from museums that appear to value sales so highly. Online stores, whose links are visible on the home page, certainly emphasize cultural consumerism. It's a fine but drawable line;

most museum professionals, including patrons, admit the importance of the store to the bottom line as well as to the reputation of a well-rounded institution.

BASIC RULES

There are a few basic rules of good branding. The virtual store, like the physical one, must reflect the museum's brand through its selection of merchandise and pricing. Just because there's room on a Web site for a limitless inventory does not give license to stock brand-inappropriate items. And because the screen is flat like a page layout, the traditional branding techniques of logo, theme lines, and type and visual consistency hold sway. The online stores represented in this chapter do a praiseworthy branding job with an impressive variety of digital tools. Any museum, of any size or budget, can employ the same tools.

Mid- to large-size art museums have the budgets, and the years of experience, to produce fine Web sites and online stores. They've done the pioneering that any small museum can build on. What they do in hundreds of pages the small museum can do on a much smaller scale. A southern art museum has developed a template that's useful to study. This is no trinkety gift store, but an outlet for desirable items that fit comfortably under the museum's halo. All the typical logo items—T-shirts, mugs, and baseball caps—are designed in the museum's gray and red logo colors. Visually, the online store has a "look," something often lost in actual stores. The store has commissioned ties and scarves "inspired by" works in the museum, and the works are pictured beside the merchandise. All the arts pervade the museum store site. Links at the top of each page invite site guests to visit the local symphony orchestra, a major theater company, and a prestigious art school.

Surprises fly out of every corner at a Midwest art museum, and the Web site easily captures that energy. It is one of the few sites sensible enough to use the animation capability that every Web site is born with. This movement and energy establishes enough goodwill to carry the visitor through a large menu of merchandise. The variety of gifts echo the museum's collections, from craftsmen's vases to children's water color kits. A list of art books, alphabetized by artist, makes for easy selection and reminds the visitor of the breadth of the museum's collection.

Trust a major museum of art to brand its online store with encyclopedic information. At the bottom of many of the pages that display the museum's strong collections, this link appears: "Visit our Online Store for related publications, reproductions, and other products." The Major Art Museum is a smart brander, understanding the synergy between seeing art and purchasing a memento of it. The Web is a great leveler, and even small museums can stock impressive stores. Many a store manager who bemoaned not having an online presence has acquired one within the year. It's a wise move because, whether shopping or buying, visitors can feel a personal relationship to the artifacts and the museum that offers it. Relationship is the beginning of loyalty. Online stores, even more than actual museum stores, give visitors time to contemplate and associate. Predictably, this online store is stocked to the virtual ceiling with a range of attractive objects, mostly of the book-CD-jewelry-tabletop variety, and the quantity keeps visitors at the site. One muses about which painting features the pink pearl brooch, or which surrealist the curved paperweight refers to. The site has you hooked. Store and museum have collaborated to make you think about the vast resources of its art, which is, after all, what its brand is all about.

LINKING TO THE REST OF THE MUSEUM

One Midwest children's museum knows how to put shopping in its place. Its online store is linked to the museum by matching merchandise to exhibitions. So one clicks on the "Food: How the world grows" and gets a full range of culinary merchandise. Nothing scrawny about this site. Not only is the merchandise novel, there are links from the store back to specific galleries where the food exhibition is mounted. Each store page is filled with exhibition-related animation, so the food merchandise page has a growing plant, and the sailing ships exhibition shopping site features billowing sails. The visitor's acquisitiveness is satisfied, but their thirst for the museum isn't; visit the online shopping site and you'll want to dash right down to the museum to see more. The shopping site also links to a teachers' site where learning plans, tied to the exhibitions, are available. Never once does the children's museum forget what its mission is.

The shops at a Mid-Atlantic house museum also remain true to the museum's mission. Divided into sections such as Garden Shop, the Parlor, and Heritage Hall, each item is accompanied with a description of its materials and function that places it in its period. The dignified brand image is maintained and the mission of education is advanced.

RETURN VISITS

A West Coast museum uses its online merchandise as a loyalty-building feature. The first page of the electronic emporium features gifts for the current month, so that if visitors don't see something of interest right away, they know they can return for another look. Web sites are so easy to update, it makes sense to rotate products regularly. Timeliness is another unique feature of the Web, and items can be put out on the digital shelves the minute the weather changes, or the very day an ethnic holiday begins. The "New for you" showcase has its own button on the home page. And upon arrival at the store page one sees: "We've created this section to showcase the newest merchandise additions to our site . . . a quick peek for our frequent visitors."

The store also related its items to lectures and events throughout the museum. For example, the Programs site announced a talk on art glass, and, sure enough, glass bowls and vases were featured items in the online store. Many museums advertise memberships on the store page. After all, it's the place where that popular member benefit, the 10 percent discount, takes effect.

Links to Membership, or Volunteer Opportunities, or Lectures are the equivalent of posting a notice on the bulletin board of the local bookstore. The store is a place where people gather. But caution is necessary. A poster in a bricks-and-mortar store might take up 5 percent of the shopper's view. A display line on a Web page is more intrusive. A good designer will organize elements on a Web page so they occupy the proper amount of space in the layout of an online store. The square footage of any one store page is too valuable to the brand to clutter with distracting messages.

OPPORTUNITY TO SPEAK TO SCHOLARS OR SENATORS

Obviously, mass-market visitors aren't the only audience the Web site reaches. An advantage the online store has over the store in the museum lobby is the huge potential audience reach of the Internet—future visitors, prospective donors, scholars, lenders, trustees, curatorial job seekers, civic leaders, government, and the media. If they're already visiting your site, there's a chance they might click over the store, a further opportunity to appeal to their interests. Just as you would merchandise an actual store for this range of visitors, give the Web pages of your online store an appearance that welcomes their interests. A simple way is to organize the books according to interests, and let visitors virtually wander to the section that intrigues them. It's a powerful way to show the range of your mission.

ONE STEP AT A TIME

Web sites start small and build, or change, at the need of the museum. The following branding suggestions can be implemented at any time, and any one of them strengthens the branding.

Open your store site with one item that makes a statement for the store and the museum. It could be a book cover, toy, houseware item, or reproduction. A curse of the store's home page is what layout artists call fly-specks—lots of little photographs on one page. They're not big enough to stop the shopper in the virtual aisle, so sweep them away. There are some specks indigenous to shopping sites, like the shopping cart icon and multiple purchase links. And the museum's logo. It belongs on every page.

Merchandise that is relevant to your mission belongs on the store's home page. Select one main visual. An example not to follow is the small art museum that led off its store site with a large enough image, but of a book about horses. It was irrelevant and confusing. Members of the staff, working with the Web designer, can select items that best express the museum's personality. If you want to offer more items, organize them in categories. The Newport Mansions online store stocks tableware, furnishings, and accessories reminiscent of Gilded Age Newport. And the Web site says just that, perfectly underlining the museum's image. Stores that categorize their stock with links like "History for Kids" or "Victorian Garden Supplies" put the emphasis back on the museum. Use mouse-over panels to tell stories relating the merchandise to your mission. The Wing Luke Asian Museum does this very well. Some museums physically connect from gallery to store, with a discreet link. This doesn't have to smack of consumerism. You could link to a book or an educational kit that continues the education begun in the galleries. Conversely, link back from the online merchandise to the appropriate exhibit.

REMEMBER THE OFFLINE STORE

Sites that show a lot of merchandise take on a life of their own, divorced from the museum. To emphasize the fact that the online store isn't just a catalog, but a part of the museum, show a photograph of your brick-and-mortar store, too. It needn't—shouldn't—take up a lot of space. Find an aspect of the real store that's photogenic and it will communicate even if it's a small photo. Just like actual stores, utilize the amenities of technology to include a message card, with the museum's logo or a signature visual, and messages that read "For your home from our historic home," or "Happy Graduation to the future scientist." Your electronic card could also include a brief description of the item and how it relates to the museum.

Electronic emporiums don't stop at the traditional gift-giving occasions. There's room for dozens of new holidays that are especially meaningful to the individual museum. By inventing Moon Shot Day, Sacagawea's Birthday, or Tapestry Appreciation Month, museums spike interest in their specialty and give it a tangible boost.

Even in the limitless spaces of the Internet, stores run out of merchandise. Or more serious to customer relationships, the visitor leaves the site without purchasing. To forestall this, offer a museum membership as a consolation and reason to come back. The offer might read: "If you don't see anything you'd like, we'll be happy to send a gift membership to the recipient of your choice." Because so many Web site visitors click to the store, it's an excellent place to suggest membership, and to once again reiterate the mission of the museum.

Shopping locations have a long history, with origins in ancient marketplaces where information, as much as merchandise, was traded. Today's online stores serve similar purposes. A click of the finger is a stroll to another stall, and down that path lies a whole new world of information. A museum could offer a real service to elementary school educators by offering downloadable lessons based on books or learning materials from the online store. Other downloads that teachers would appreciate are photographs from books or artifacts in your collection. Of course, accompany any photos with a description and credit line that mention the museum, just as if it were a photograph sent out in a press release.

The online store can collect information, as well as dispense it. Use part of the order form to collect other names and broaden the reach of your message by asking, for example, "Who else would like to know about the lore and lure of our region?" As you collect the names and add them to your database, remember to include a field for the referrer. That person is obviously a loyal museum friend and should be targeted for special attention when a new exhibition opens or a special program is offered. Remember that if you recruit new visitors by e-mail you should include an opt-out check box.

Order forms are useful for collecting other data. For example, "How did you hear about this Web site?" or "When did you visit our museum?" (always call it by name, of course!) or "Which exhibits would you like to see more related merchandise for?" These survey questions reinforce the museum in the mind of the respondent at the same time that they're polling opinions.

Staying with the marketplace analogy, the online store could lend some of its space to constituents it wants to do business with: civic leaders selling tickets to community events; not-for-profits promoting, say, a walk-a-thon; cultural organizations selling tickets to performances. Choose your partners carefully, and don't become the wall for just anyone to paste their poster on. It's your site, and the recommendation will be seen as an endorsement, so tie-in with a group whose mission complements yours. Keep the other organization's logo discrete and don't put up too many promotions at one time.

Local colleges or universities are especially apt tie-ins, and the learning section of the online store might announce course schedules or lectures that augment your mission. Undergraduate schools also supply interns, volunteers, and research capabilities, plus the ad hoc specialists who can be hired to update your Web site, sew costumes, or edit brochures.

Becoming a source for information is another way the store can connect visitors to your brand. Many books, and certainly periodical articles, would never earn a place in the limited space of a real store, but online many items can be stored in the electronic back room. How effective it would be for an art museum to comment on, and link to, an exhibition review from the local paper or a more general article from an art journal. Collecting and posting other people's articles gets museums into the blog business, and it's a lot of work without an intern or volunteer; that said, it places the museum in a broader context and enriches the brand.

The virtual store never substitutes for the real one just off the lobby.

Distance shoppers should always move into the museum itself, to experience the full force of the brand. Offer downloadable gift certificates online for fulfillment in the actual museum store. With the museum's name, logo, and address on the printout, it serves as advertising while it's sitting on the kitchen counter waiting to be redeemed.

Sound doesn't get enough of a hearing on Web sites and the technology is there, just waiting to be called upon. Online stores can use music and sound effects to build interest, just as actual stores do. Animals roar in zoos, birds chirp in botanic gardens, and pianos play in period parlors; these evocative sounds don't have to stop at the door to the store. Music designers play to consumer behavior by scheduling livelier tunes after lunch and oldies so shoppers will linger in the aisles to listen. Without resorting to expensive play lists, you can borrow from the concept. Utilize the time visitors spend at the store by playing brand-suggestive music. Branding experts use the term "storytelling" when defining how a brand makes itself manifest, and you can certainly tell stories about your merchandise through music. Don't forget the best sound in the world, the human voice. Casting a person from your staff to talk about the merchandise forges an indelible connection between the brand and the souvenir.

Other bells and whistles combine sound and visuals, and electronic stores can use motion to even greater effect. A technically precocious intern with some free rein can make brushstrokes appear in an art museums store, fish swim in an aquarium's store. The cursor is also available to carry the museum's personality, to literally carry it around the site. Cursors don't have to be arrows; they just have to be small enough to stop and point to small targets. A cursor can take the form of an arrowhead or a quill pen nib. It can turn into one of those symbols at each click. With shoppers clicking all over the store pages, the cursor will be quite visible and available for branding. It's worth asking a computer techie about the possibility. If budgets, time, and clarity do not allow for elaborate effects, it's relatively easy to introduce motion in the form of a pop-up logo.

And, to further impress shoppers as they click over a site, some museums are packing their sites on laptops and taking them to the shopper. One big-city natural history museum set up its online store, on a laptop, at the local airport. The museum had a small counter at one of the concourses, with a display of gifts that could be purchased online. An attendant helped visitors access the site. Offsite kiosks attract waiting passengers, entertain them, and reestablish a popular tourist destination for return visits. The display kiosk itself is especially effective now that many people travel with their own laptops.

■   ■   ■

Online, as offline, the museum store is an invaluable extension of the interpretations begun in the galleries; it is an engaging reminder of the museum's mission and brand. Like the actual store, it is a place where visitors reflect at leisure about the museum, and let entertainment augment education. Engagement, reflection, and entertainment all contribute to a visitor's ability to absorb the experiences of the museum and remember their meaning.

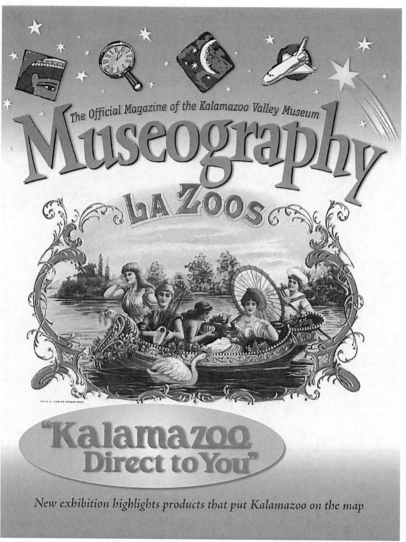

The Official Magazine of the Kalamazoo Valley Museum

Museography

LA ZOOS

"Kalamazoo Direct to You"

New exhibition highlights products that put Kalamazoo on the map

Museography, *the official magazine of the Kalamazoo Valley Museum, targets a diverse audience, and the magazine reflects both the variety and excitement of the museum. Each issue offers a children's game, a feature that will keep the magazine around the house for a while. The calendar of events brings the museum into the home. On several pages of the magazine, a small boxed announcement, titled "Ask the KVM," invites readers "who have a question about a person, object, or artifact that relates to the history of the southwest Michigan area" to send it in. And again, the reader is involved in the brand. Courtesy of the Kalamazoo Valley Museum.*

14

Publications

Publications serve multiple marketing purposes, beyond their primary goal of news and information. To prospective visitors, they market your museum; to members and donors they reinforce the loyalty. Where advertising is efficient at acquiring new visitors, story-rich publications retain members. Call it retention, or relationship marketing, publications engage and involve readers, month after month, bringing a sense of the museum into the home and making exhibits, programs, staff, and mission a part of your constituents' lives. They are potent tools for keeping your name in front of your public, strengthening your brand and forging lasting bonds.

Publications are held in the hand, shared, and passed along. They have weight and heft; they feel important. When mailed, they are delivered right to the home, or business. Periodical publications arrive regularly, reminding people of the museum. Inside these timely missives are feedback devices in the form of letters to the editor, mail-in surveys, or change of address cards. In the familiar format of a newsletter or magazine, fundraising events are announced, programs are listed for registration, contributors are recognized, and volunteers are enlisted and acknowledged.

Before addressing how each of these relationship builders can be realized in a newsletter, magazine, or book, you need to assess who is on their mailing lists. The four major groups that will benefit from publications are prospective visitors, members, donors, and internal markets such as volunteers. Sometimes, a publication is the best way to reach important subsegments such as seniors. Magazines bring the museum to them. Other groups to target are people in the community, government officials, scholars, and collectors. For the latter audiences, museums might splurge and print one-time publications such as books and catalogs. All these groups need to be reminded, with varying degrees of regularity, of your brand. Larger museums utilize a mix of magazines, newsletters, catalogs, and books. A limited budget, and good story ideas, will carry the message in one effective piece.

To begin the process of deciding what to publish, in what form, and how often, study your lists. If you have these databases stored, you're off to a good start. Some typical list categories are members, visitors who have signed in at the front desk; purchasers at the store; ticket holders for events; guests at the restaurant; people who have written, e-mailed, or telephoned for information; and donors.

Next, evaluate your information by sorting the names into "behaviors" such as: live locally; contribute regularly; attend programs; bring friends; donate; volunteer; influence the community; have clout with government; support you in nonmonetary ways; live out of town but support the museum through memberships, donations, or purchases; provide social or business connections.

No list is ever complete or good enough, so determine how you might create new or update old databases with a guest book at the front desk, the purchase of lists, lists shared with other institutions, or an advertising or PR campaign directed at name gathering. There's a treasury of ideas in other organizations' publications, and one museum consultant collects stacks of them to cull for ideas. Museums of any size can make a wish list and then check with their printer to see what's feasible. The other invaluable partner in periodically mailed publications is the U.S. Postal Service, whose representatives are happy to sit down and discuss shipping issues such as weight in ounces, bulk rates, prepaid, presorted, and forwarding-address-requested.

With these facts in place, you're ready to make decisions on the type and frequency of your relationship-building publication.

MAGAZINE OR NEWSLETTER

The differences between magazines and newsletters are significant, but not mutually exclusive, and not necessarily hinged on cost. Magazines tend to be bigger, splashier, printed on heavier paper, and cost more to print and mail. They use a lot of color, and boast lengthier articles and crisper photographs. Newsletters are usually shorter, less expensively produced, printed on lighter paper stock, and less expensive to produce and mail. Many museums deploy newsletters to their larger, less committed audiences, and magazines to their more preferred lists.

Magazines by definition are a storehouse of many subjects. Their articles go into depth, and tend to broaden the scope of the museum. Readers peruse magazines for enrichment. In the wider world, magazines are enjoyed curled up on the couch. Newsletters are by definition newsy. They telegraph time-sensitive news about exhibits, the calendar of events, recent donations or acquisitions, and volunteer information. Their parallels are daily newspapers, read at breakfast or on the commute. Both magazines and newsletters shout your museum's personality. Both types of publications have a name, type style, and format that are distinctive to the museum. Both display the logo large and often.

Emotionally and psychologically, magazines appeal to those who will think about your museum; newsletters speak to those who will act. Magazines are meant to be savored and kept. Newsletters are read quickly, their calendars or announcements perhaps cut out and stuck to the refrigerator door. The newsletter has many similarities to a magazine, but is quite different in tone and attitude. Instead of in-depth, they're on-time. Where magazines are deliberate and often reviewed by peers, newsletters are immediate and usually researched by one person. Elegant writing is often traded off for succinct writing. Each publication appeals to different psychographics or behavior types, which might reside in the same person. When planning when and to whom to send a publication, remember that sometimes we feel like a magazine, sometimes we feel like some news.

MAGAZINES START WITH INTERESTING STORIES

Articles in a museum magazine, whether long and inclusive or short and chatty, tell stories that reflect the personality of the museum, and will have a tone of voice—serious or witty, erudite or folksy. A simple rule of stories is introduce something provocative, be interesting, and have a conclusion. Explore story ideas that complement your mission, not just echo it. Don't feel constrained to treat only your artifacts, your building, and your programs. Use quotes in your articles. Here's an opportunity to embed the perspective of experts.

SUBHEADS

If your story gets long, utilize subheads.

FUSION OF WORDS AND VISUALS

Appoint an editorial committee, an ad hoc one is fine, to brainstorm story ideas with a fresh slant. Quarterly magazines, especially, will become burdensome if left to just one person. Even the most experienced writers will assure you that good ideas emerge more reliably through the mechanics of a group discussion. Once a robust idea is agreed on, the actual writing is relatively easy.

The photographs, frequently left until the last minute, ideally should be considered first. Because magazines linger on the coffee table, and frequently on the tabletops of higher-level donors, they require first-rate photography. The photo and the story idea take shape together; if there's no good visual, there's no story. When it comes to costs and time of staff, one arresting, assigned photo and a brief caption is more efficient than a long story fly-specked with some leftovers from the archives.

Use visuals as often as possible, even at the expense of words. Photographs communicate quickly and with great relevance, so a shot of an exhibit immediately identifies your museum. Then look outside the walls for photographs to accompany longer, in-depth stories. Use the medium of a magazine for beautiful, professional photography that deepens the image of the museum. When laying out the publication, make the photos as large as possible, so they have impact and import.

Make the cover count. A major strength of magazines is the high impact of an 8½-by-11-inch cover and that always requires a professional photograph. Magazines can be displayed with other publications in the bookstore racks or on counters. Take advantage of this placement and present a well-designed face to the public. If your magazine is mailed in an envelope, design the envelope to be as graphically interesting as the magazine inside. Kalamazoo Valley Museum publishes *Museography* with a cover as lively as the rush of content inside. The shooting star design that bursts from the banner also appears throughout the pages and, with sparkling brand savvy, in the banner at the top of every Web site page.

NEWSLETTERS

In the marketing mix of ads, brochures, Web site, events, and newsletters, newsletters could be the most effective choice for connecting your audience to your museum. They have reach and frequency; they reach a lot of people often. They're retention tools, maintaining interest among the customers you already have.

Like newspapers, they provide information that's current and helpful and, by highlighting a new exhibition or program, they offer good reasons to return. Giving a seasonal slant, which newsletters can do through stories and images, puts the museum in a new perspective. Calendars, with their current listings, are a staple of newsletters, and the fact that they change regularly demonstrates how dynamic your institution is. Special activities, like a members' trip, use the newsletter to list itineraries, prices, and deadlines. The news format imparts a cachet that promotional mailings lack. There's a double advantage in that you can float a prospective activity and get a sense of interest in advance. Newsletters, because of their timeliness, are places to list telephone numbers that are in effect for special programs. They are also effective mediums for feedback. Surveys and questionnaires provide information not only to the institution but to the reader. A farm museum may not need to know its readers' views, for example, on sustainable agriculture, but a survey plants concepts that reinforce mission. Survey results also supply community reinforcement when soliciting foundations or government agencies for funds.

EXTERNAL APPEAL

Because newsletters arrive, unbidden, in the mailbox, they could be perceived as junk mail, especially if they're sent as a self-mailer. Newsletters, once folded, lose all identity. The side with the mailing label is frequently as dull as a bar code. Prevent this by designing an attractive address panel and repeat the newsletter banner, or the museum's logo, on the address panel. There's still space on that panel to flag some of the stories inside. It's more expensive to mail the newsletter in an envelope, but it will stand out. If you display newsletters along with brochures in the lobby or store, keep the cover side up, not the side with the mailing label. Instruct the printer to leave, say, one hundred copies unfolded.

What's inside is a potpourri of information: one big news story, one human interest piece, the next month (or quarter) calendar, a just-for-fun feature like a puzzle or a game, and a reader-response device like Q&A, or letters to the editor or the suggestion box. Envelopes can be "tipped in" (stapled) for contributions. Standing columns, which readers recognize

CHAPTER 14

from one issue to the next, aid continuity. Just as in magazines, lots of visuals are important, and they can be illustrations as well as photographs. To be avoided are computer illustrations, which are too generic. Pay an artist for one or two signature illustrations, ones that symbolize the museum, and use them throughout the newsletter for "color."

Because of the immediacy of newsletters, some visuals might be maps or charts. Photography in newsletters, unlike magazines, favors news, not depth; however, that does not mean amateurish, and a few guidelines will produce professional-looking photos. People shots are terrific if you can see all the faces, so they should be head and shoulder shots. Keep the number of faces per photo to four or less, leaving space to incorporate a prop, one that identifies the event, or the museum. This could be a sign in the background, a handheld artifact, or a piece of wearing apparel as simple as a campaign button. Select your lead, front-page story for its photogenic qualities, and then get a relevant photo. Don't make the mistake of one environmental newsletter that featured bicycle travel as its main story, and then accompanied it with a photograph that didn't have a bicycle in it.

FEEL THE PAPER

When you have the advantage of putting something in people's hands, don't stint on paper. Specify the heaviest weight you can afford to mail. The type of paper conveys your personality, and a glossy finish communicates a different image than does a speckled stock. If you consider a color stock to give more oomph to a one-color print job, select the color with an eye to your logo, colors within the museum, other printed pieces, and your personality. If, for example, your logo uses primary colors, a black on pale blue paper stock would convey a totally different image. Note that there are a wide range of recycled and environment-friendly stocks.

PRINT SHOPS ARE YOUR FRIENDS

Coordinate the activities of your designer and printer. Customarily, designers select their own printer. However, it's also customary for a not-for-profit organization to have a pro bono or cost-only printer among its donors. On target, on time, and on-budget newsletters and magazines rely on the cooperation between designer and printer, and you may have to play matchmaker. Together, the creator and the executor decide if the job is a self-mailer or contained in an envelope. They compare the effect and cost of 4-color, black and one color, or black and white; weight of paper; number or folds; and size of sheet. The face of your publication is so important that it should be discussed at the time of the initial design. If your magazine is mailed without an envelope, you'll save in postage; however, you must allow space for a mailing panel, postage permit, bar code, and return address. Printing and postage costs vary wildly and your printer should know all the postal regulations; if not, it's best to find a printer who can navigate these waters.

Beware, and this can't be cautioned too often, of freebie print jobs. Sometimes a good price is possible only because the printer has an unused supply of paper and some unexpected free press time. The paper could be the wrong finish or color for the museum's look. If the stock is too heavy, what you save at the printer will be eaten up in postage. A wedged-in job allows little time to do traditional press checks.

ADVERTISING

Magazines and newsletters with large mailing lists are appealing to advertisers, and the money made by selling space is tempting. Before running other people's messages, a few cautions are worth noting. A magazine's primary purpose is to build a relationship between the museum and the member, and any other brand will conflict and confuse. Publications have scant control over the look of the ad, which could clash with their own style. Publications have the right to deny space to incompatible advertisers, but that requires written guidelines and an ability to say "no."

THE BANNER NAMED UPDATE

Names of publications are as significant as people's names, and "Update" is the John Smith of periodicals. Use this highly visible part of the publication to herald, dispatch, or give clarion call to the museum. Create a newsletter or magazine name that tells readers immediately what museum is issuing it. That part of a newspaper that carries the name and distinctive typeface is called the banner, and it boldly conveys identity and pride. The Illinois Central Railroad History Museum calls its newsletter the *Green Diamond*, after its most famous line. The Block Museum of Art, in Evanston, Illinois, keeps its public informed with *Around the Block*. Both render distinctive all the updates inside.

PUBLICATIONS VS. WEB SITES

Much of what gets communicated in printed periodicals is covered thoroughly in a Web site. But there's a significant difference. The interactive Web is an active medium, requiring the reader to pay a visit. Magazines and newsletters come right to his or her mailbox. Virtual information commands a huge place in our world, but there is nothing like a quietly tangible piece of paper. Handheld, saved, and then passed along, newsletters and magazines are intimate and easy to identify with. Readers keep them for easy reference. And as these delightful pieces of mail sit on kitchen counter or desk, they quietly flash their names and reinforce yours.

BOOKS AND CATALOGS

Books and catalogs are nonperiodical publications that raise the reputation of a museum far beyond its family of members and donors. They enhance the brand immensely by dint of their scholarship and also because they look as substantial as the expense of time and money required to produce them. Books are full-length treatises on subjects of broad interest that will shine a new light on a museum's brand. However, many a museum has found that the prestige of publishing does not pay back in brand burnishing or money. One museum administrator admitted that they made a big mistake in self publishing the wrong title at the wrong quantity. It's easy to be persuaded into publishing the book of a friend.

Select the books you publish with care, not just to their content but to their relevance. It may seem obvious, but make sure that the book's subject matter corresponds to your museum's primary collection, mission, era, geographic parameters, size, interpretation style, scholarship level, and target audience. And flaunt the museum's name as publisher. Although established brands in the world of publishing can afford to be discreet, listing their names politely at the bottom of the title page, with only their logo on the spine, museums can't afford such modesty. A designer and printer are good allies in blazoning your name. Then, of course, the book doesn't just sit on a shelf in the museum store. It is arranged in a display, with signage.

GRAPHICS

Think through the visuals you would like to complement the text of your book. Many authors will approach you with proposals that perfectly match your mission, but don't include recommendations for illustrations, photographs, charts, or maps. Creating and producing these elements will affect the schedule, cost, and appearance of the final product. More important, they dramatically affect the meaning of the book and its relationship to the museum. Consider the photograph of a settler with a plow in a rocky field: it would adequately depict the mission of a museum of history, or farming, or natural sciences. It might blur the picture of your museum. Discuss visuals with the author for his or her ideas. Bring in a visual person to brainstorm at the very outset. One good candidate for this idea session is the person who designs your brochures or ads, who will understand strategy as well as the creative and production aspects of "illustrating" a book. The easy solution is photographs in the archive, but be prepared to crop photos so you zoom in on only the most salient image.

Catalogs are encyclopedic by definition, and in itemizing the objects in a collection, or the works of a single artist or creator, tend to de-emphasize the institution that authored the catalog. Make sure your museum gets credit as organizer of the exhibition and print the credit line large on the cover. For more brand identity, include a letter from the museum president or director, introducing the catalog and tying its subject matter to the museum's mission. Sign the letter with the writer's name and title and museum name. Don't forget a big signature, the John Hancock effect.

GLOSSARY OF PRINTING TERMS

Working closely with your printer will improve your newsletter or magazine immeasurably, and save time and money. Here are some terms that will bridge the language gap.

4-color—piece is printed in full color. This is the most expensive color printing process and gives the most realistic look. The process uses four inks—red, blue, yellow, and black—in various combinations.

3-color—usually black plus two colors. It has a rich and elegant graphic look, usually where there is no photography.

2-color—usually black plus one color, where the type is black and the one color is used for accent. This can be effective in highlighting your logo or other features of your publication that emphasize your image. If black is not one of the colors, be sure that one color is dark enough for the type to be read easily.

1-color—usually a dark blue or green that can be used full strength for type and screened back for background photography.

Banner—the name of a newsletter or magazine. It usually appears in a strip at the top of the page and is understood to include not just the name, but any illustration or graphic treatment that is a consistent feature of the name.

Bindery—how the pages of the piece are bound together. Saddle-stitching, or stapling, is the least expensive way, and perfectly adequate for smaller magazines. *Time* magazine is saddle stitched. Perfect binding is for large publications, like *Fortune*. Spiral binding is an inexpensive option with the look of a professional manual or workbook.

Bleed—an image that fills a page to the edges.

B/W—black and white. What newspapers use. It gives an editorial or documentary look. Black type on white is the most legible.

Captions—these lines of copy accompany every photograph, and not just to identify the photo. Captions under photos are always read, and you can put important information here that might not be read in the body of the story.

Cropping—cutting away parts of a photograph so only the most important part shows. Designers frequently crop out some of the sky, ceilings of rooms and table legs, or artifacts that are not part of the story. Cropping is done electronically, never with scissors.

Die-cut—imagine a brochure where the top is pointed to resemble the roof line of a court house, or a booklet with a square cut out of the cover that reveals an artifact pictured on the inside page. These shapes have been cut with a die, a tool much like a cookie cutter, and the process is expensive, especially if the cuts are special. For example, if the brochure were cut to resemble a unique roof. The cost of a die-cut might be less expensive than 4-color printing, and give your piece similar impact. It's one of many options available in the printing process.

Dingbats—small graphic designs that punctuate a layout. Designers unanimously prefer proprietary designs to the generic starbursts or lightbulbs found on the computer. A logo or signature illustration, used in a small size, is very effective as a dingbat, especially at the end of a magazine or newsletter article. It's an easy typesetting technique that adds brand consciousness on every page.

Folds—how the printed page gets folded is part of the design, and is an extra cost of the print job. For example, if you want your newsletter folded into its 4-page, 8½-by-11-inch size, it will be printed on 11-by-17-inch paper and folded once. Some newsletters are printed on broadsheets that are folded twice, vertically and horizontally. There are other options, depending on the size of the printing press. Indicate this to the printer or you'll have to fold it yourself. If you want some copies of the same newsletter folded into thirds for mailing in a #10, standard size envelope, indicate that on the print order, as well.

Illustration—original drawings. Used effectively where the real object doesn't exist yet, as in a new building, or isn't photogenic, as in computers. Even food can sometimes be represented better in an illustration than in amateur photos. Illustrators have distinctive styles and if you find one you like and can afford, his or her work can give your publications a strong identity. Amateur illustrations are best avoided. Illustration is not usually an economic alternative.

Indicia—the preprinted stamp in the upper right hand corner of a printed piece that indicates your mailing has been prepaid. The post office provides you with a number and the printer sets the type and prints it. Having an indicia allows for bulk mailing rates.

Page layout—graphic designers take all the text that has been written, all the photographs that were selected, any illustrations, charts, maps, or graphs that have been drawn, and assemble them on a page in an easy-to-follow arrangement. This organization of material is called a layout, and there are many ways to lay out a page for maximum impact and clarity.

Paper stock—paper comes in an almost limitless range of stocks, varying by weight, thickness, texture, finish, and price of paper. The look and feel of your paper is significant for your branding effort.

Photography—the most realistic look. Photos can be cropped for more clarity, interest, and impact. They can be inexpensive if the amateur photographer knows what he or she is doing. Photographs of people or buildings tend to look generic, so make sure the subject matter relates strongly to your museum. Professional photography can be expensive because the costs include the photographer's day rate, model fees, possible location fees, film, and preparation of digital files. You will, however, own the photograph and can use it whenever and wherever you please.

Pull quotes—segments of the text or a quote that are repeated in a larger type size, often with a border around it, and placed outside the column.

Saddle-stitch binding—magazine pages that are bound together with staples in the fold.

Stock illustration—illustrations whose copyrights have been sold by the artist, usually to a stock photography company that, in effect, rents them to a marketer for use in ads, brochures, posters, Web site, or any of thousands of other uses. These are usually of mediocre quality, distained by designers, and not to be confused with stock photography.

Stock photography—these are photographs whose copyrights have been sold by the photographer, usually to a stock photography company that, in effect, rents them to a marketer for use in ads, brochures, posters, Web site, or any of thousands of other uses. The price of stock photography is based on usage, including what medium, how many people will see the image, and how long the image will be seen (weeks? years?). Stock, also called royalty-free, photography is considerably cheaper than original professional photos, but not exclusive to the buyer. It is not uncommon to see the exact same photograph in two different ads, for two different advertisers. A charming snowy trail through the woods was once spotted for a state tourism ad and an insurance company retirement ad, both in the same newspaper on the same day.

Text Box—when a short article or information subordinate to the main story is separated out from the main text, it is set in a box, often with a tinted background. The text is then said to be boxed with a screen.

Trim—where the printer cuts the paper at the end of the printing run. The pages will be cut to the exact size specified, for instance, 9-by-12 inches. If your type or images are too close to the edge, you run the risk of getting trimmed.

Typeface—the style of type, such as Goudy, Garamond, Helvetica, or the standard computer face, Times Roman. Once you select a face for your publication, stick with it. It's part of your brand.

Type font—the entire range of characters that are needed for most printing jobs, including alphabet letters, upper and lower case, numerals, punctuation, special characters, and symbols.

Typesize—type is measured in points. For example, 10 pt. type is the typical size for text, depending on the typeface. Anything less than 6 pt. is hard to read. Text set in 12 pt. type looks like a child's book and amateurish. Once you get into 14 pt., 16 pt., or 18 pt. type, you're talking headings or subheads. Don't be afraid of using 28 pt. or 36 pt, or larger, in printed materials where you want the concept to really stand out.

Orange is the color of the Racine Art Museum. Visitors see it first in banners that flag the building. With great consistency, the color reappears in the lobby and its brochures, the museum store wrapping paper, and even the plinths that support gallery display cases. Photo by the author.

15

Audio Tours

Branding by Script

Technology has greatly reduced the cost of producing audio tours, so much so, in fact, that museums that never considered them an option can now do so. It can't be stressed too forcefully that scripted audio tours are excellent branding tools. Assuming that there's enough storage space, time of staff to dispense and collect the equipment, and that they're not too ostentatious in a small museum, audio scripts, announcers, pacing, sound, and technology help interpret your exhibits and heighten visitors' understanding of your brand.

They will never replace a good docent. Wands and headsets continue to be the second best guide available, but they are miles ahead of a nonexistent or unskilled tour guide, and as museum hours increase, and volunteers decrease, they're worth a listen.

AUDIO TOURS ENHANCE BRANDING

The value of audio tours goes beyond interpretation to a dynamic impact on branding. Structured tours keep visitors moving through the galleries of the museum, so they see as much of your establishment as possible. The average museum visit lasts twenty minutes! The more time visitors spend with you, the better your opportunity to build a relationship, and audio tours hold visitors in the museum longer, engaging them in your story. In large museums, the hour-long audio tour condenses a vast experience into one that's more embraceable.

In museums of every size, the recorded tour, through the narrator, embodies the personality of the museum. This unseen voice must be compared to the other voices of the museum. The guides who represent the museum to the public in person may come from the ranks of educators, curators, volunteers, or your donors. By all rights, they should reflect the personality and brand of the museum. But being real people, guides frequently represent their own personality and their own culture, to the detriment of the museum. Guides can appear too youthful or too mature, overly staid or improperly casual, not scientific enough or too erudite. A professional voice on an audio track overcomes a lot of visual misunderstandings.

A good audio tour is emotional. It makes visitors feel happiness, outrage, awe, or surprise, the feelings that help them not only hear the facts, but grasp the overall concept. This is good for learning, and wonderful for communicating the mission. Audio scripts start with a concept—the mission—and build a compelling narrative from there. The feelings conveyed by story line, tone, narrator's voice, and sound effects must be consonant with the personality of the museum. A visitor will feel emotionally quite different upon leaving a Holocaust museum than after a contemporary art museum or a botanic garden, and audio heightens that.

HOSPITALITY AND THE AUDIO TOUR

Like a host greeting a visitor, the audio tour can start the visit on the right foot. Whatever hurdle a visitor had to cross—crowds, too much to see at one time, variety of subjects that aren't of equal interest, unfamiliarity, or just distance from the parking lot, they can be easily deflected with the warm, skillful charm of the voice on a wand. The voice reinforces the decision to visit and outlines what lies ahead. Of course, real front desk personnel, guides, and guards do the same thing, but a scripted voice does it reliably and with the authority of the whole museum.

Audio tours permit talking time, those precious moments when people share their observations. Human guided tours leave little time for discussion, the give and take of information so necessary to a meaningful visit. The digital narrator should urge visitors to press the pause button at any time and discuss their impressions with their companions.

Voice-over announcers have the gravitas to deftly maneuver through, or around, exhibits that might be offensive, inappropriate, or just difficult for some audiences. As questions of censorship and public responsibility are asked ever more loudly, careful answers are needed and these can be tendered on a recording. Sometimes it's simply a matter of scholarly exhibits and these, too, can be handled less awkwardly by a reader who never stammers or blushes. A tour doesn't have to be controversial to dismay a visitor, who may have come to see something else or not understood the exhibition. Then the voice of authority can succinctly explain the strategy behind an exhibition, validating it so that even a disinterested visitor comes away with a real respect for the museum.

Where precise use of language matters, prerecorded tours guarantee that foreign and scientific words will be pronounced correctly, along with multisyllable terms, and recondite English expressions, too, for that matter. Digital scripts can go a step further by offering the option of a full explanation of a term.

Americans with Disabilities Act (ADA) requirements for the hearing impaired state that museums should provide hearing devices or interpreters, and that need becomes more pressing as aging baby boomers storm museum gates. Audio tours fulfill a legal and moral requirement and, in the process, embark on sound public relations.

Areas under construction, those walled off galleries that disappoint so many visitors, can be finessed by an audio tour. When exhibitions are being installed, or taken down, they can still be heard, described in vivid detail. In fact, audio tours are a good medium for promoting any upcoming attractions, and summarizing departing ones. Off-limit galleries are holes in a museum's story, and audio tours can keep the learning and the image whole.

Of course, a lot of learning gets interrupted by those information fanatics who, on a live guided tour, comment constantly and ask questions without remorse. And few guides are knowledgeable enough to parry the questions of a genuine scholar. Audio tours can solve that learning gap, too, by programming information in several levels.

With audio tours you can record in-depth information, or refer the visitor to other sources. This attention to scholarship greatly augments your brand image, and this section of the script might be used for other lectures or presentations.

There are physical limitations to consider, too. A docent can walk a group only so far and this, while allowing better pacing, sacrifices a feeling for the whole museum. With a voice guide, visitors will cover more territory. No tour guide, real or virtual, can make a room less crowded, but an audiotape can make the visitor feel he's in his own space. Crowds are an upside-downside situation, good for revenue and socialization, bad for individual reflection. A headset, especially, gives a visitor a sense of intimacy with the exhibits, and the quiet needed to connect with the museum itself. Small museums have an opposite problem—tours shorter than the standard forty minutes and no crowd dynamic. The imagination of audio in this case conjures up space, providing additional commentary and a little sound to expand small tours into richer ones.

Ironically, a real person can give too much personality to a tour, at the sacrifice of the institutional personality. Narrators, however, are perceived as spokespersons designated to deliver the institution's message. It's important that someone do so, and the audio guides comply with grace. Live tours frequently end with polite group applause, a chorus of thank-yous, handshakes, and individual conversation. This is the socialization and group dynamic that all museums want. However, the ending message, which summarizes the tour and its relevance to the museum, frequently gets cut off. The taped announcer's thoughtful recap of the museum's educational mission is heard.

The branding advantages of an audio tour are many. An appropriate voice with a scripted message perfectly conveys the spirit and distinctiveness of the museum. Scripting guarantees consistency of message, the sine qua non of branding, which even the best roster of docents can't guarantee. Branding also requires that visitors reflect on and relate to the museum; the ability of the tape to pause lets visitors do just that. The tangible equipment itself—a wand, booth, and collection depot—provides surfaces to brand the museum. The obvious expertise of an audio lecture enhances the museum's image. And with minor programming software, a visitor can type in his or her name and opt into the museum's database. The visitor can even key in his name and tour the exhibits while the narrator directs his comments to "Tom."

As museums build their databases and identify the characteristics of a museum loyalist, they consider the competition, as well: just who and what compete for visitors' time. Entertainment always shows up. Audio-taped guides, with vivid scripting, dynamic acting, and bell-and-whistle technology, are more entertaining than most person-guides. The stage is set for the branding messages.

Educationally, prescribed audiotaped tours are the surest way to present the material in the context the curators envisioned and are consistent with the museum's mission. And, there are educational advantages that aren't evident at first, but are even more compelling, starting with a more dramatic story to amplify learning. Diverse audiences demand that museums take a whole new look at tours, in terms of content, structure, and delivery. Scripted yet flexible audio tours can adapt learning to different segments and levels. Imagine a one-hour tour specifically designed for African-American, Hispanic, or Native-American students. Envision it adapted for different grade levels or language proficiency. Think how an in-museum tour could be repurposed for distance learning.

When it comes to school tours, what all young people have in common, of course, is their youth. They grew up on MTV and gaming, and are used to entertainment models for all communications. This group has quick intelligence and their energy doesn't suffer a slow pace. Audio guides allow for the unstructured pacing that help agile minds learn. Tapes and hand-held devices are familiar formats and may even add reassurance in strange surroundings. And all generations of museum-goers have been familiar with audiovisual. A + V, it is widely acknowledged, communicates more effectively than either one on its own. The see-hear combo is powerful indeed! Museums, with big stories to tell, unfold them in all their glory when sound is partnered with visuals.

There are also internal uses for audio guides. A well-told story will also inform your staff, and everyone from guards to curators to donors should be invited to take the tour.

PRODUCING AN AUDIO TOUR

Once a museum decides to investigate using audio tours, there is one essential step to take before making the call: know what you want to include. An audio tour for adults lasts about an hour, for children no more than thirty minutes. While that seems like a long time, long enough to cover many topics, an effective audio tour is focused. It might talk about one exhibition, or a theme threading through many exhibits, but it is never a list or catalog of the whole museum. If there are several areas to be covered, they should be addressed in separate tours.

Production of an audio tour enlists the services of a writer, producer, announcer, and engineer. The steps and timing are as follows:

1. **Preproduction.** The writer and producer visit the museum and research the material that will go into the script, including the exhibits, artists or creators of the artifacts, the museum itself, and background material on the exhibitions. The writer will sit down with museum staff to agree on the mission of the museum, the focus of the audio tour, and the desired response a visitor should have at the end of the tour. At this point it is wise to ascertain the approval process: who is responsible for giving the go-ahead for each step. Preproduction takes about one week.

2. **The script.** The writer will prepare a first draft in about a week, with sound effects and music indicated. When the museum approves the general outline, the writer and producer start casting announcer voices. It's important to have voices in mind because scripts are meant to be heard, not read, and "hearing voices" will help move the approvals along. Most projects take two rewrites. Depending on approval time— and this is a museum's function—the script stage takes about two weeks.

3. **Production.** The producer, engineer, and writer record the script. Depending on the number of voices used, this can take several days in the studio. Unless you're recording in a city with a lot of theaters and a large pool of actors, it may take longer if talent isn't available.

4. **Postproduction.** It takes about one week to rough edit the voice track. Music and sound effects are then added. Music is usually pulled from royalty-free stock music libraries, and the search for appropriate existing music and arrangements can take some time. Composing and recording original music will take two to three weeks and is costly. A rough mix of the voice track, sound effects, and music is sent to the client for approval. After that, the final mix, where all elements of the sound are balanced, is made. This step, assuming quick approvals, takes about one week.

Then the master recording is produced, duplicate copies are made, and the total soundtrack is sent to the wand or headset companies for installation.

The sequence of production may vary depending on the museum, but the development process is standard.

SCRIPT AND WRITER

Of the four experts involved in creating an audio tour—writer, producer, voice talent, and engineer, the writer is the most important. Everything flows from the script; it delineates the structure of the tour and then fills out its tone and mood. It is at the writing stage that the personality of the museum is agreed upon and captured. Many museums find it difficult to pinpoint just what their brand image is and professional writers are adept at helping them find that distinction and articulating it. The script is the roadmap of the tour, dictating its length, subjects covered, and points made. Working with the writer helps uncover the motivations of your target audience, and the best way to communicate with it. It's tempting to write the script in house, to take advantage of the large supply of knowledgeable, articulate, creative people working there. There are pitfalls though, and you should know which people will fall into them.

Who Shouldn't Write a Script

Marketing staff—these writers are excellent communicators, but they're too positive. They're trained to emphasize the good points. A strong audio tour will tell the whole story, warts on the reptiles and all.

Curators—these writers are skilled and accurate. However, they're too wordy, accustomed to in-depth treatises geared to scholars. They can't write to the general public.

Directors—these writers understand the museum brand, but they see too much. They understand the broad picture and can't focus on a themed, one-hour tour.

Docents and education department—these communicators function effectively in a give-and-take format. They're accustomed to talking, not writing.

Most museum professionals are steeped in their subject, having absorbed knowledge over long hours of intensive work. They have trouble condensing their information for people who must come away with that same level of appreciation in one hour or less.

ANNOUNCER

Professional announcers, like actors in movies, plays, or commercials, bring the story to life. They keep the narrative moving, not to mention the minds of the visitor who is listening to it. Announcers' voices reflect the mission and brand of your museum, and their voice is the second most important part of the audio tour. You will listen to audition tapes, male and female, to select the voice. This is a new skill that will be difficult at first; most people hear voices without analyzing their effect. Insist on auditioning until you feel comfortable with the voice.

Avoid the second temptation of hiring nonprofessional voice talent to save money. Amateurs cost twice as much as pros, according to one writer, because they will go through twice as many takes in the recording studio, stretching a one-hour session to two hours. Sessions are billed by the hour. Amateurs also produce the vocal clicks, spits, and whistles that must be cleaned up by the editor—at double the editing time and cost.

Plan to use more than one voice, for variety. Even the most compelling voice gets boring after a while, and visitor/listeners will tune out. Whatever the concept of the tour, it probably covers a variety of exhibits, perhaps eras or geographical areas, and probably a selection of artists or makers. It makes sense to vary the voices that describe all that.

The primary narrator can be a male or female voice. Much depends on the focus of the tour. If it describes the activities of whalers, a New England male voice would tell the tales admirably. The voice of the women who wait behind could also carry the scenario. A good actor of either gender will communicate strength, creativity, adventure, or whatever your concept calls for. Always, it is the image of the museum, the brand that finally dictates the sound.

The cost of professional announcers will vary by locality. Many state and local laws require use of union talent, and audio tour production houses comply. Some states, like Arizona, Florida, Georgia, Iowa, North Carolina, and Virginia, are right-to-work states, and can hire anyone they want, including professionals who don't charge at higher, union levels. It's something to consider when selecting a production company.

PRODUCER AND TECHNICIANS

The entire project of an audio tour, from concept through delivery to your door, is supervised and coordinated by the producer. Companies that produce audio tours will assign a producer to your museum. It is this project supervisor's job to hire and oversee the timeline and budget. He or she coordinates the writers, announcers, engineers, recording studios, editors, and music houses. He or she is the contact person for the museum, and the one you will work closely with. He or she facilitates the transferal of tape to wand or headset, and all deliveries. You could produce your own audio tour, and hire the other professionals yourself. If you've already gone through the process, and understand the commitment of time and talent, this is definitely an option.

MUSIC

Music is essential to any audio production. Think of a radio commercial without music—and they last only sixty seconds! Music is a branding tool and a responsible interpretive device. An audio tour accomplishes its goals better with some degree of music to propel the story. It sets the tone and literally underscores the overall concept. It cues the narrative by announcing when something important—or funny, or harmful—is about to happen. Music adds real content, like how a harpsichord or call-and-response sounds. Instrumentation can indicate a move to another gallery, or a change in time period. The expenses of music start with research to find what seems appropriate. It ends in the editing, fitting the right sound to the right visual.

Music costs vary widely. Most museums purchase stock music, compositions that have already been written and recorded. Their copyrights have been bought by stock music libraries, which means that the lyric writer, music composer, arranger, and musicians have signed away their rights to collect any royalties. You will pay a one-time fee for a stated use of the music. For example, you will pay a contracted price to use the music in head-set delivered audio tours, at a museum which admits 50,000 visitors a year, for a period of two years. Theses numbers are negotiable, but once established, very firm. If, for example, the museum decides to waive entry fees, and the number of visitors doubles, the stock music company may raise your price. The contract must be renewed after the stated time period. You can't reproduce the tour as a cassette and send it to schoolrooms, or sell it in the museum store. Music contracts are friendly and fair, and enforced.

If you decide to produce original music, the costs include composer, arranger, musicians, and studio time. Music for a one-hour audio tour is a lot of music, and very costly. However, you can negotiate to own it outright. Payments and royalty fees are complex enough that it is strongly advised to hire an entertainment lawyer who can review any music contracts quickly. Lawyers' fees are small compared to surprises down the road.

Sound effects are relatively inexpensive to buy. Many are available on consumer CDs, of course. An endless selection can be found in stock music or sound effects libraries, for a negotiable fee. The greatest expense will be time of staff to research accurate effects, and any search fee the stock library charges. Consider, for example, the sounds of water. Is it the Atlantic Ocean which is rough and wild, the Caribbean which is calm, or the lapping ripples of a harbor? Water sounds may need to be complemented with sounds of gulls, macaws, foghorns, or buoy bells. Details matter, and not only because they so powerfully augment the educational content of the tour. They matter because even a slight confusion on the part of the listener distracts from the message. And details contribute positively to the content. Deploying sound effects effectively throughout the sound track takes a certain amount of experimentation, as scholarly accuracy doesn't always communicate the message as well as a less accurate sound might. Professional engineers conduct trial and error efficiently and as part of the postproduction editing and mixing process it is included in the hourly cost.

Depending on talent, studio recording time, music, sound effects, editing, and quantity, a one-hour audio tour will cost $5,000 to $20,000. As technology continues to streamline production, costs will decrease.

IN SUPPORT OF REAL PEOPLE

The alternative to a recorded message is a real person, and they cannot be replicated. Museums would be the last institution in the world to deny the supremacy of human contact in learning and community building. People, in their limitless individuality, make connections, bridge divides, discover new answers. It is an irony of the twenty-first century that the robustness of the American lifestyle, which has powered the explosion of museum attendance and thus the need for more interpretation, also lures away to competing activities those same people who might fill the job. Along with this surge, the pressure on museum staffs continues unabated and they cannot be expected to take over guide duties, too. Technology, fortunately, is no longer the domain of techies alone, and its creative, friendly applications are ready to tackle traditional jobs.

The Lobby

First Impression and Last Impression

There's no grander entrance than the approach to a museum. Think about the plazas and parks, streets and stairs visitors have navigated to get there. Finally the doorway is breached and the goal is in sight. At this point, it looks like a great trip, or a chore. The lobby is the visitors' first impression and everything they think about the subsequent exhibitions will be built on the preview.

The lobby is also a transition zone, from everyday routine to adventure. Most visitors, being neither scholars nor experts, consider the museum a special place. For some it commands respect and awe. For others it leads to exploration. Many use museums as meeting places or vacation activities. Many college students speak quite sincerely of museums as places of learning, challenge, and achievement. Whatever exceptional role museums play, their lobbies are ramps that accustom and acculturate and ease the timid into the main galleries. As staging areas, lobbies let people look at others and learn how to act.

All this space for looking, assessing, and planning is essential to brand building. People need to understand the product, in this case the museum visit. They must think about it and its relevance to their lives. They should find other visitors they relate to, get input from them, and reinforce their decision to make the trip. They should hang out with the product, have fun with it, and laugh over it. If the visitor is tired or hungry, the product will suffer. The museum lobby is a decompression area between the known world and the new, giving visitors time to make the museum their own. A brand must be received by the consumer, as well as delivered by the marketer.

As branding tools, lobbies set the tone for the institution. Marble pillars and monumental stairs convey one image. Bright lights and colors convey another. A large information desk, populated with well-dressed volunteers, sends a message, as does a plain counter staffed by college kids. Some reception counters practically block the entrance, while others are a football-field's length away. The impressions these give can be imagined. Whatever experiences unfold beyond, they will be set up by the lobby experience. Ideally, the lead-in will perfectly presage the experiences to come.

Following are some foyer features that all museums should consider when making a first—or last—impression. Some can be implemented or modified. Some are locked into the architecture. All can be ameliorated.

MATERIALS—MARBLE, WOOD, GREENERY

When all museums were marble, the communication was clear. This was a place for the elite, whether in net worth or brains, a cathedral with a direct line to Culture. Some museums still look that way. And others work the other way, with a direct line to the people.

If the entry is glass, the message is transparent. "Welcome, welcome! Take a look around. Go to the rooms that interest you." These are museums that meet their guests at the door, with no butler intervening. Most twenty-first-century museums, holdovers from the other century but having to expand, now compromise. The old lobbies remain grand and awe-inspiring, and that's appropriate. The new wings are brighter and more people-friendly, and that also defines museums. Queens MoMA, the temporary home of New York's Museum of Modern Art while its Manhattan building was being reinvented, was all glass, its lobby leading visitors past the lures of the museum store, with exhibits in plain sight. It was editorialized extensively as the harbinger of museums to come, the image of hospitable openness.

Moving from the grandeur of marble to the elegance of wood, some lobbies don't fare so well. The many museums that started life as stately mansions now look just dated, rather than privileged, out of kilter for the contemporary layouts and installations that many genres of museums now utilize. They don't foreshadow the exhibits to come. Of course, not all mansions and their boskiness mislead. House museums that honor an individual's success and his or her involvement with art and culture wear their carriage trade lobbies well. The Frick Collection in New York and the Isabella Stewart Gardner Museum in Boston both echo expertly the personalities of their namesakes.

VISTAS

Lobbies should be more than collection areas for entrance fees and bag checking. They should be vantage points. The lobby of the Field Museum in Chicago does that. The first exhibit seen is the iconic Sue, the dinosaur that is now almost the logo of the museum. Enter this museum and you know it's about natural history. The long, railroad-station configuration offers a quick glimpse of all the other exhibitions branching off in galleries on either side. Even museums in older buildings with awkward layouts can provide a view by placing artifacts in the corridors, by the stairs or elevators, or in the stairwells.

Ten Chimneys museum, the rural Wisconsin country home of Broadway legends Alfred Lunt and Lynne Fontanne, is accessible only by guided tour, so its lobby is the only place where visitors can explore on their own. This reception area opens onto several galleries that are delights of interactive exhibits that give visitors the freedom of exploration both before and after the guided tour.

The promise of exhibits to come would seem to be no problem for a botanic garden, and the Chicago Botanic Garden does indeed greet visitors with lush vistas. However, until the visitor physically traverses great distances to a wetland, a Japanese Garden, a lily pond, or a prairie, it's just a pretty panorama. To explain what's out there, the Garden places a surprisingly small exhibit at the entrance to its lobby: five glass vases, each with a stalk of flora, and a simple white card to describe the plant, grass, or flower. This human-scale exhibit is part of the brand of this celebrated museum.

The greatest viewing lobby belongs to the San Francisco Museum of Modern Art. Right at the doorway one can see across the lobby to the upper floors, to a colorful glimpse of the art ahead. In fact, from the sidewalk, passers-by can look through a large window and see the museum within. Off the lobby is the restaurant, a reassurance of sustenance at the end of the tour. The lobby has been compared to an older-era market-place, a place to look around, socialize, and acclimate.

WELCOMING COMMITTEE

People play many roles in a museum, none more important than at the door. Uniformed or T-shirted, standing or seated, they represent the brand in ways human visitors can readily relate to. Conversely, sometimes these janissaries don't represent the museum well at all. At one elegant mansion-style museum, the ticket-takers sat at a folding eight-foot table, crossed legs visible, conversing almost without pauses. One receptionist was a senior, well-dressed and coiffed. The other was a young person, in baggy black attire and wild locks. It was hard to tell what the museum stood for. At another mansion, the guardian at the gate was an elderly man, standing at a podium, overwhelmed by incoming crowds and look-ing unnecessarily hapless when ticket stubs started falling. One got the impression of a falling down museum, when in fact it is an effectively delightful one. At a contemporary art museum in a large city, the ticket squad at the entrance counter was a group of young people in diverse dress, presenting a well-trained yet creative face that perfectly prefaced the exhibits beyond. At many small museums, the store clerks double as the cashiers. These people are so knowledgeable and involved, they perform the introductions perfectly.

Living museums get it. Being greeted by a costumed, trained actor with a script tells the visitor exactly what to expect. Frequently, these welcomers will guide the time travelers to the next exhibition and answer questions at the end of the trip. If the aim of the museum is to show how earlier societies interacted with each other and their environment, the "lobby" experience establishes the mood at the beginning and reinforces it at the end. The greeters at the Portland Art Museum also put a human face on the institution's content. Wearing sashes, or medals, or headgear appro-priate to the featured exhibition, they transformed a temporary exhibition into the museum's own. This is no small feat in the museum industry, where several brand names share the same traveling content.

It goes without saying that the best lobbies are staffed by impeccably informed welcomers who understand that information is not *about* a museum or its exhibits. Information *is* the museum. The people at the lobby desks are the first link in a long chain of interpretive experiences and, in most cases, they are the most sensitive link. They interact with the visitor when he is most confused and they must, in a few moments, convey the mission and persona of the whole experience.

SIGNAGE

Here's where visitors learn why they came, where to go, and when to return for future exhibitions. Signs tell where the restaurants and restrooms are, because people need to be comfortable before they can learn. Signage, because it is visual, also reinforces the museum brand. Large posters of the current and future exhibitions telegraph the mission. Size and placement of signs also give insights into the museum's personality. One big-city museum places signs for its multiple dining areas in stanchions on the floor, framed on the wall, and in banners hanging from the ceiling. Another major-market museum features items from its store in large banners over a sales counter that faces the main entrance. One could argue that signs sell too much and bombard the newcomer's mind with too much information. However, signs are meant to be read, one at a time, at the reader's discretion. Each sign slowly adds detail to the image. Many lobbies miss opportunities by not filling their over-large spaces with clues about what goes on within the massive spaces.

MUSEUM STORE

Most museum stores are located, wisely, in the lobby. At the beginning of a visit, their wide selection of books and postcards provide a preview to the works inside. At the end of a visit, they summarize the experience, giving the mind-overloaded visitor a place to review and make sense of what was seen. Most museums, mindful of the profits from stores, locate them near the front doors, so customers can shop without paying a museum admission. The Musee d'Orsay in Paris takes this a step further by allowing entrance to the museum through the store, thus avoiding lines. In small museums, the first person seen is the museum store assistant, and these staffers are invaluable in propounding the brand image at the outset of the visit. Their helpfulness at the end of the visit, when purchasers are collecting memories, puts the final bow on the brand experience. Store personnel who understand the merchandise and its tie-in to the exhibits will function much better as ambassadors of the brand.

Where space allows, museums place satellite stores in kiosks, near the galleries. Some see this as commercialism, the better to sell more stuff. They can also be seen as interim lobbies, places where people can pause, meet, and talk about the exhibits. Many experts agree that museums need more space for thinking, not just for viewing. When it comes to maintaining a brand, customers have to be allowed to experience the product. With museums, that means thinking about it.

CHAIRS

Another accessory to thinking, along with space, is comfort; not enough attention has been paid to seats. Chairs and benches allow visitors to catch up with each other, wait for the tour to begin, rest up for more viewing, or watch others for visual clues to behavior. The Whitney Museum of American Art has a few benches in the lobby, and more in stairwells where people also can gather or reflect. Ten Chimneys' lobby has lot of couches, an art-deco chaise, and some art chairs. Many museums have placed reading tables in public spaces throughout the galleries, where visitors can literally collect their thoughts on paper. Anywhere there's a chair there's an opportunity to reflect and reinforce the brand. The Milwaukee Art Museum has one of the larger proportions of banquettes to square feet of lobby space. It also graciously allows schoolchildren to lie on the floor and gaze at the Santiago Calatrava umbrella roof.

REFRESHMENT

The culture army also marches on its stomach. The mind creates new connections more efficiently when the body is satisfied. Placing the refreshment area in the lobby helps visitors refresh their minds, as well as their bodies, and continue thinking well after the motivating experience has ended. Chicago's Adler Planetarium has a huge cafeteria off the lobby, offering an unequaled view of the city's skyline and sky. Tables and chairs are essential when the visitors are children, especially if the museum ticket is an expensive one and the visit includes more than one stop. The lobby location keeps the rest of the visit in plain sight. The Toledo Museum of Art spots snack bars at several entrances, with signs at the tables encouraging resters to reflect and imagine. The Long Beach Museum situates its restaurant on a terrace overlooking the ocean, and the entrance is refreshed by salt breezes. For museums that are on a campus or in a far-flung part of town, lobby cafés put the museum on the map. Without this reminder of refreshment, visitors might too quickly associate the museum with remoteness. Where there is a restaurant, no place is strange and everybody feels they can belong.

ARTIFACTS AND DISPLAYS

Lobbies may be transit zones, but they can whet the appetite for what's inside. A well-placed display proclaims the brand. In the Vietnam Veterans Museum in Chicago, the first sight, and a dazzling one, is a ceiling sculpture made of thousands of hanging dog tags. This is a powerful, edgy museum—in concept, content, and location, and the assault starts right at the beginning. At the National World War II Museum in New Orleans, visitors are confronted with a very large tank. At the entrance to the Utah Museum of Natural History, the lobby contains display cases with bug, beadwork, and rock exhibits. One understands the scope of these museums' missions immediately. Even small museums have scope and their small reception areas can give a sense of the collection that's in storage. All it takes is a small, wall-mounted display case that highlights an artifact of the month.

Technology, because of its interactivity, personally welcomes each individual to the lobby. The seductiveness of a computer can steal the limelight, so you might want to set aside a special place. There are limitless ways to enhance the museum, beginning with a short "about us" movie. Visitors can select their routes, explore a given exhibit in detail, leave comments, and send e-postcards to friends. It's a private way, in a public space, to collect visitor study exit interviews and other kinds of research. Instant memberships, offered at the moment when visitors are most involved, can be handled without any sales pressure by a screen and a keyboard.

Donor walls are an integral part of lobbies and they should reflect the brand as carefully as does the rest of the décor. Formal brass plaques are traditional, acrylic nameplates are newer, and the "wall" might be a column, screen, or window. A workshop of metal, wood, stone, and composition materials are available to connect philanthropist to museum. One not-for-profit organization has a garden of sculpted flowers occupying a quarter of the lobby, each bloom the name of a contributor.

ASCENDANT PUBLIC SPACES

A major portion of most lobbies is the stairs, which can either invite or turn off. All museums, large and small, can ameliorate their staircases. The Metropolitan Museum of Art owns the best outside stairs in the world, filled as they are with people happy just to be sitting at the Met. Any museum with stairs should encourage this sort of casual familiarity. The stairs at the Seattle Art Museum mimic the steady climb up from the harbor for which Seattle is known, but the museum's climb is easy and filled with sights, a store, and a small coffee area along the way. The staircases at the National World War II Museum are designed to twist and rise, turn and descend, mostly in shaded light. The museum doesn't try to simulate the steps of a military invasion, but the arduousness is a reminder. At the Getty in Los Angeles, the steps are outside, leading through gardens and to the impressively large research buildings. It is this entire campus that represents the Getty's identity. Of course, at the spiraling Guggenheim in New York, the lobby and its staircase is the building. More than an architectural design, the stairs are an adventure, as are most of the exhibitions. A stair lesson can be learned from the National Gallery in London. Here's another venerable building, with permanently high stairs leading to the galleries. But these steps are inlaid with ceramic tiles that paint pictures and tell distracting stories, all the way up. Any museum could paint the risers on their stairs, too.

Stairs are transitional spaces, leading from outside to way in, and they don't have to be wasted space. One museum puts artifacts in cases at each landing. Another offered naming rights for every public space in the building, including the stairwells. At every step visitors understood the community pride that distinguished this cultural center from all others.

CURB APPEAL

As with residential real estate, how a museum looks at the approach can make or break the sale. And you don't have to be Rocky's Philadelphia Museum of Art, high on a hill, to stand out. There are other imposing public spaces and it doesn't hurt to shoot for them. To reach the Children's Museum in Chicago, one traverses the lively walkways of mile-long Navy Pier, a galloping fun urban mall of shops, theaters, river cruise boats, sculpture, and a Ferris wheel. The brand is prefigured half a mile away.

Sometimes just cutting a new path to an existing structure provides a brand-building introduction.

This would be nothing more than academic musing if there weren't really bad physical introductions to museums. The worst lead-in to a great name has to be the route one takes to Tate Britain, a four-block walk from the nearest Tube stop, a poorly marked journey that's best navigated by following people who look like tourists. The city and the museum should have figured out a better-marked approach. The same caution applies to the smallest museums: don't let your space be buried by the town around it. The civic leadership owes you that much, at the very least.

BRANDING OPS

The lobby is a visitor's first impression, and last impression, of the museum. This is the first chance the brand has to make itself known. It's also where the brand can make a strong farewell-and-come-back statement. Like photo ops that offer a snapshot of an event, branding ops in the lobby give a snapshot of the entire museum:

- Chairs in the lobby, for meeting, familiarizing, and reflecting.
- Printed material about the exhibits, placed on restaurant tables, coat check counters, and display racks at the museum stores.
- Well-trained lobby staff, calling the museum by name.
- Admission buttons that visitors are encouraged to keep. Even if they toss them when they get home, they'll keep the image of the museum out front for a while.
- Graphics for the front of the information counter. These often-massive structures will look less forbidding with branding.
- Floor graphics. Supermarkets have discovered this surface for promotions, why not museums?

Cincinnati's Contemporary Art Center is a striking architectural personality with an enduring community personality as well. Comment cards, placed in the galleries, invite visitors to suggest additional items for a curated exhibition. This is a brand whose core values are open-mindedness and participation. What the exterior doesn't reveal is the sloping staircases within, inviting visitors to walk from floor to floor—a slanting parade that is an exhibit in itself. Photo by the author.

Loyalty Eating

How Art Museums Reinforce Their Brand Image at the Dining Table

Consider all the reason why people like, need, and go out for food, and you'll understand why the museum's image can sizzle or go stale on the strength of its restaurant. The restaurant's nourishment reaches far beyond hungry people straight to the brand of the museum itself.

Since every aspect of the museum, from exhibits to bookstore, must do its part in the battle for the consumer's heart, a good place to start is the stomach. Nothing in a museum nurtures loyalty like a café. It doesn't have to be a full service restaurant; at least one large museum has what amounts to a catering truck outside the entrance. There's a difference between feeding visitors and nourishing them, and branding speaks to the latter.

Spending time with the product is one of the first ways a customer is encouraged to buy and buy often. A purchaser has to look at the product from all angles, try it in different circumstances, walk away from it and approach it from a freshened perspective, discuss the product with friends. Time, however, is something museums don't have. According to some studies, the average museum visit is twenty minutes, hardly enough time to register the exhibits, let alone form a lasting impression of the museum itself. Here's where the restaurant comes in. The restaurant gives consumers a place to relax and refresh, discuss and ponder, and reattack the museum with renewed interest. Very few places in the museum offer this reflection space. In many museums, the restaurants possess the only chairs in sight.

A conveniently located restaurant, preferably indicated by signs in the lobby, assures visitors that, should they tire, physically or mentally, there will be resuscitation. A snack break could very well extend the visiting hours, increasing the time a visitor has to soak up impressions of the museum. Museum visitors also need comfort, and have neither the intensity nor fortitude of scholars. They need food, chairs, and bathrooms. Serendipitously, a restaurant provides all three. Learning and new synapses can begin when the creature comforts are assured.

Museum restaurants communicate the museum's hospitality, and the need for hospitality is rather new. Although visitor services have long understood the imperative to listen to visitors' needs, in today's service economy, understanding is a little passive. Today, museums have a responsibility to invite folks to stay for something to eat. Loyal customers want to really like their museums and food is, now and ever, lovable. Just like those other pillars of the community—politicians who hug grandmas and businessmen who go to school for a day—museums are expected to embrace and enfold. That's a job made to order for the café. Few other aspects of the museum hold the power to nurture. Cheerful volunteers and friendly docents are a start, but for good, old-fashioned loving, nothing fulfills like something from the oven. It's strange, really, how many museums eschew this basic wellspring.

REFLECTION

Most important, the eating room provides meditation space. Here is where the art amateur, fresh from his brush with exhilaration, can ponder and internalize new knowledge. Under the glass tops of café tables at the Toledo Museum of Art, printed cards read: "Reasons to stop at the Coffee Bar: (1) promotes relaxation; (2) relaxation leads to conversation; (3) conversation elicits new ideas; (4) new ideas are the seedlings of the future; and (5) create your future."

CIVIC PARTNER

There's a practical aspect to food, as well as an emotional one. Museums are fast becoming part of the fabric of a community. People live in museums, attending meetings, going to lectures and films, bringing in school groups, socializing at benefits, bonding at family programs, and learning new skills through professional social services. To meet these daily needs, new buildings provide comfortable meeting rooms, advanced education facilities, and auditoriums for the community. They also include restaurants to feed the large populations who come to work and play. Unfortunately, many hide their personality. In many art museums one will find Formica tables and plastic chairs in areas that amount to little more than a food court. Some museums conceal their restaurants in the basement, or behind the museum store, or in a crowded alcove off the main passageway. At the other extreme, highest marks go to the museums that try to fortify visitors at every opportunity. Big museums can afford restaurants and cafeterias and some plant satellite cafés in the corridors around blockbuster exhibitions.

Even small museums use their one-of-a-kind facilities for catered events or business lunches. One major museum even set aside a room as a club member's room for Sunday brunch. As museums join in the life of the community, they have a nonpareil opportunity to advance their brand by breaking bread with its workers and leaders. And dining venues are so easy to promote to the community. Sending menus to offices, retail stores, and colleges will garner incremental awareness and goodwill, along with lunch customers. Small budget companies will appreciate off-site facilities for meetings, new employee welcome lunches, and retirement parties. The brand, of course, plays a visible role in the business lunch setting, and visiting diners should see brochures on the table, artifacts on the shelves, and the museum's mission on the wall.

Many museum restaurants are destinations in themselves, but they don't have to be MoMAs or Gettys. The Granary Restaurant at the Ella Sharp Museum pulls in customers on its own merits and is a powerful brand-builder for the museum.

A second community needs to be addressed in all museums: the staff. Management, curators, guards, and volunteers all need to be fed. More important, they need to feel a part of the institution. Though they may not use it often, the restaurant is a place where they can get in touch with each other and their institution. Gift meal tickets make nice thank-you presents. Each employee is an ambassador for the museum, spreading the fact and image of the museum to a network of family and friends. These coffee-break and lunch-hour diners are potent resources who deserve to be nourished.

In Russia, once again the Hermitage has scored a branding coup by plugging in to young people with the Internet Café. In addition to specialty coffees and snacks, computers create electronic postcards that feature a work from the museum side by side with a photo of the visitor shot by the computer's Web camera. Importantly, there are many tables set far from the computers for quiet talking.

BUSINESS LUNCHES AND CORPORATE GALAS

All institutions look to the business community for financial support, and some funds are captured literally by passing the plate. In downtown city museums, a good percentage of the meals are bought by locals, mostly businesspeople, looking for a good place to have lunch. The new Santiago Calatrava-designed Milwaukee Art Museum knew this and included in the plan a footbridge across the highway to the business district.

A huge amount of revenue comes from catered events, and while the restaurant is usually more an expense than a profit center, catered events are quite profitable. Along with the dollars comes invaluable awareness and loyalty. Businesses and other organizations like to throw events in the museum because of the quality association. Each basks in the halo glow of the other. Lest the museum's image get lost in all this radiance, museums are well advised to take several protective maneuvers. One major museum stipulates a mandatory gallery tour as part of every catered event. Another discreetly places volunteer docents wearing "Ask Me" tags around the buffet tables. At the door, the museum should prepare a standing sign that welcomes the party, by name, signed with the museum's name. There are so many ways to spread the museum's name around, from free passes in the goodie bags to brochures in the cloakroom. And the evening's photographer should be encouraged to shoot guests in front of a museum exhibit. But the food, of course, is the key. After the ball is over, people promote the places where they've had a good meal.

Since many museums now offer their facilities for events, the bar is raised to provide ever newer experiences. Having a strong brand helps because events can be themed to your unique ingredient that nobody else has. At the same time, a themed event reinforces your brand. At The Grove National Historic Landmark, a restored nineteenth-century orchard and nursery, guests drive up an unmarked lane, under canopies of trees and over a bridge, to reach the country cottage where ceremonies and dinners take place. And although few venues can equal the Heller Aviation Museum's landing strip for arriving wedding parties, many museums can arrange carriages, hay wagons, or safari vehicles. Any museum can invent party occasions that celebrate the brand: harvest moons, the house owner's birthday, or Groundhog Day.

FELLOWSHIP OF THE TABLE

Despite the prominence and goodwill enjoyed by museums, they still can be intimidating. After all, any respectable interpretation or education is by definition "new." But eating lunch is a great common denominator and the object is to get a fork in the hand of people who don't usually visit museums. In some museums, the tables are shared, and that's a wonderful opportunity for visitors to form relationships around the experience; literature or table tents are great conversation starters. The social aspect of museums reasserts itself with informal cafés where it doesn't take more than a coffee machine and pastries to get people talking. It might be informative if, once in a while, curators or education directors came by, much as chefs step out of the kitchen, to greet the guests and listen.

NIGHTS

Young people's Friday night wine and cheese parties open the floodgates to all kinds of after-hours fun. On Friday nights, one museum welcomes young working families with children, groups that don't have many daytime hours to get together. It's such a friendly, personal experience that many kids come in pajamas. Evening events needn't stretch the budget and it doesn't take a lot of money to bring in a platter of cheese and crackers, or cookies. For museums that now include theaters and evening performances, the food bar is an appreciated extra that patrons will probably pay for; the combination of physical, intellectual, and hard-working nourishment is very brand-enhancing. Only for large museums? Not at all. Small museums can work this moonlight intimacy to special advantage.

The location of a museum restaurant aids in branding. If near the lobby, it is part of the first impression the visitor takes in. If one walks through exhibits to reach the dining room, additional brand impressions can be made. At the San Francisco Museum of Modern Art, for example, the restaurant is not only off the lobby, but visible from the street. It's like a retail store and invites stopping. It also assures the foot-weary that there's a place to regroup and extend their experience. Even if visitors leave after eating, the restaurant is their last impression, sending them away full of good brand associations.

Museums need strong brand images to compete for audiences and loyalty. In an economy short on leisure time, and long on leisure choices, the museum restaurant is a powerful decision-making tool.

From a branding perspective, one could argue both ways between a restaurant name and the museum name above the door. Yet, even simple meals are a special interlude, and special names feed into that. Consider the Café a la C'Art, Big Shoulders Café, Chakula Café, and Prizm and the personality boost they give to the Tucson Museum of Art, Chicago History Museum, Caldwell Zoo, and Museum of Glass. It's good branding to satisfy hunger at a memorable place.

BRANDING OPS

Any one of these simple branding opportunities augments the larger brand activities throughout the museum:

- Art or reproductions in the dining area remind diners where they are and what they saw. Printed material describing the artifacts provides table talk.
- Service staff trained with a simple, "Thank you, I hope you are enjoying your visit to the Museum of. . . ."
- Printed receipt with the logo or tag line of the museum included.
- Maps of the museum on the tables or checkout counter, making it easy to return for another look.
- Signage throughout the museum announcing the location and hours of the dining facilities.
- Small, specialty food items for sale, with the museum logo affixed, to keep the memory alive in the kitchen cabinet.

- Crayons on the table are a staple for families with children; you could add some coloring pages depicting items from your collection.
- Table tents announcing future exhibitions.
- Menu copy that describes selected exhibits.
- Unobtrusive brochures announcing catering possibilities for private or business groups.

Everybody who leaves a museum store with a purchase is a walking billboard for the brand. A well-designed shopping bag is a smart investment. The National World War II Museum has created a graphically strong and brand-perfect extension of its image, for all the world to see. Courtesy of the recently renamed National World War II Museum, New Orleans, Louisiana.

18

Your Building

How Museums Build Their Brands Brick by Brick

Whether you're building a new wing or remodeling a gallery, it's a good opportunity to depict your brand and flaunt it. Blame or credit the star architects for raising the profile of architecture, the truth is that everyone today loves buildings. If the building project motivates discussion, or even argument, all the better, for your name is being mentioned and associated with exploration, vision, and change. Though a structure is not the only manifestation of a museum's brand, it is undeniably the biggest, and any work done to it raises awareness. Use the construction opportunity to shout your brand all over town.

The first job is to relate the purpose of the construction to the brand. If you're adding a school bus parking area, it's because so many students want to learn about your singular story. Suppose it's simply a repair of the front steps; announce that you're returning the steps to their original look, as they were when your mission was first embodied. If it's a big, architectural undertaking, be sure to relate the philosophy of the design to your distinct image.

DESIGNING A THREE-DIMENSIONAL LOGO

Think of your building as a big logo, one that identifies your museum to a wider audience and distinguishes it in a tangible way. Strangers on the street will know about you, in addition to the museum-going public. And you can merchandise your big building in many small ways. It might appear on your brochures and signs, either as a photograph, an illustration, or a graphic simplification. It will, if you send out press releases, probably be pictured in local newspaper articles. Postcards with its likeness, which are inexpensive to produce, can be offered free to visitors who will be happy to help you spread the word. Even a small remodeling project will have an architectural detail, like a distinctive window or roofline, that can be illustrated for marketing materials.

FOCUS GROUPS—MORE THAN ANSWERS TO QUESTIONS

The first tools used in new construction are purely intellectual, the analysis of your needs. All the budget in the world will be insufficient to solve all your space woes, so draw up a wish list. Assemble the staff and let everyone propose his or her best-case scenario. The second steps are more difficult; this is where you home in on your brand and its perception. At this point you'll want to research visitor attitudes toward your space and perhaps feel out community opinion. More critical is reaching internal agreement. Brand definition is customary when discussing marketing and now you'll have to visually define yourself in the context of bricks and mortar. Simple questionnaires or focus groups will help assess public attitudes toward the museum and its spaces, and how those attitudes might evolve. Conduct your research with a variety of groups: the museum family and friends, visitors, advocacy groups, educators and businesses in the community, local government representatives, and the trustees.

Ask questions such as, "From looking at The Smith-Jones Museum building, what kind of place do you think we are?" Get others to define your visual brand with: "What one architectural feature of The Smith-Jones Museum do you like best?" Get a sense of how people use the space: "In what part of The Smith-Jones Museum do you spend most of your time?" Focus on specific needs by saying: "The Smith-Jones Museum will, of course, comply with ADA requirements. What physical impediments should we be aware of?" Finally, trust children to give you the most creatively apt suggestions. Ask them to draw a picture of The Smith-Jones Museum.

Not only will you get informative answers but you'll give out some advance publicity. Every person who attends a focus group will hear firsthand about the project. They'll be insiders, with information straight from the museum itself. Even better than learning from a museum staffer or outside facilitator, they'll be hearing from others in the group and will leave the session with an interesting new subject to discuss even further with friends. If your respondents simply complete a questionnaire, they are still getting a preview. Everybody you interview will be a word-of-mouth spokesperson for the new venture.

SELECTING AN ARCHITECT

Although big-budget museum renovations have raised their architects to superstar status, it is neither necessary nor recommended to raise your new building on the foundation of celebrity. The sole criterion for picking an architect or developer is his or her understanding of your personality and brand. Architects are trained to listen to mission statements and to work with you in creating a housing that reflects your image. You must be able to communicate with your architect, confer frequently, and work collaboratively. If you think there won't be a "co" in every interaction, collect another short list to interview.

Investigate architects who have worked on widely different kinds of buildings and judge how each one fits the image of the owner. You want an architect experienced in public-use structures, but more meaningful is his or her flexibility in responding to individual situations and nuances. The interview process should include as many departments' representatives as will fit around a conference table, so the architect hears all voices. Give the staff plenty of opportunity to mull over how they use the building and let them have their say. For a museum building to have a personality, it must respond to all the persons who use it. The importance of back-and-forth talks with the architect is non-negotiable.

The national average for building a new structure is $200 to $300 per square foot, with build-outs, or interior renovations, costing less. There are as many architecture specialties as there are medical ones, and a museum that has never gone through a building project might not know which specialist to select. First timers are well advised to hire an architect as a consultant to assess the museum's requirements, draw up a list of architecture firms to interview, and help write the request for proposal (RFP). These search consultants will charge the same hourly rate their firms charge for their time, an average of $75 per hour, with the number of hours to be estimated at the outset.

If there are issues involving a parking lot or a bridge, lighting or acoustics, ecology or design, there's a right architect for the job, and the consultant can pinpoint that person. To find a consultant, ask other museums for names of architects, or contact the American Institute of Architects for a list.

When the proposals are in, the museum and the consultant will look primarily at the applicants' credentials, including what other museums they have designed. All architects are trained to analyze your unique situation and collaborate with you for a solution, and when the short list of three to five architects is determined, each of the finalists will make a presentation that (1) indicates their understanding of your needs and (2) shows proposed designs in sketch form.

It is at hour-long presentations, individually with each short-list firm, that you meet, face to face, the people who want to work with you for the next year. Since these finalists have all been chosen for their appropriate credentials, you will make the final selection based on how well they understand your brand and match it. Yes, there should be a little brand chemistry.

After the winning architect is awarded the job, the hard work of programming begins. The architect needs to know things like where the front door should face, which galleries get the most traffic, what kind of light comes through the shade tree outside. You should know things like how many offices you need, how many bathrooms, and how long visitors stay at the museum store. One of the first concerns will be environmental—the heat and humidity in the various rooms, depending on outside conditions and number of people inside.

Once the decision is made to invest in construction, branding can begin, and architects are valuable allies. Their branding savvy comes from long experience in assessing clients' needs, goals, and dreams, and they can think beyond the building to all aspects of a museum's daily life.

PUBLICIZE THE PROJECT THROUGHOUT CONSTRUCTION

For the duration of the project, your image will be one of progress and growth. Take advantage of this and publicize at regular intervals. Remember that though your project may not make the covers of magazines, it is news at home. Help the media tell the story with press releases that describe the new functions of the building, background information on the project, and statistics showing the impact on the jobs, tourism, and economic development in your community. Of course, the last paragraph in every news release is a set description of your mission and brand. All press releases should be written on letterhead that includes the most current logo and campaign line. The mailing should include a fact sheet that states your mission and captures your image. Also include a sketch of the building and start familiarizing your audience with this new profile on the horizon.

To keep the community informed and involved in the project, publish a newsletter that updates construction, previews the first exhibitions in the new space, and interviews people responsible for the new look. Submit articles to the local paper, or letters to the editor, about the positive effect on the community, and list job openings and volunteer opportunities. This good neighbor news will ameliorate any disruption in the neighborhood, satisfy the curiosity of sidewalk superintendents, and drive traffic through the building during the all-important first month, when the spotlight is on you.

To communicate more specifically with the business community, hold small breakfast seminars or hard-hat tours. These informal heads-up briefings are more than a courtesy to future colleagues; they are opportunities for sponsorships, partnerships, and memberships. Talk to business and government groups who will now have a fresh reason to appreciate your contribution to the economy. Don't succumb to the temptation to wait until the dust settles. Build on the momentum that goes with earth movers and construction cranes. Even if your project consists of little more than construction barricades and carpenters' vans, it's progress, and everyone loves the buildup.

MEET WITH THE CONSTRUCTION WORKERS

Take a new look at the hard hats working on your building; these men and women are ambassadors and new target markets, as well as prized workers. First, they got jobs because of you, and they and their families are prepared to like you very much. Second, they talk to friends and coworkers, and spread your name to a segment that might not be familiar with the museum. Welcome this receptive group with coffee, doughnuts, and family passes to the museum. Offer them guided tours of the museum and take photos of them with your exhibits as part of your press kit. For the duration of the construction, these hardworking, skilled builders are part of your brand, and you can associate their good effort with your own.

REMEMBER YOUR STAFF

Museums that understand branding will spend as much time introducing the architecture's message to their own employees as they do to the public. New construction helps bond the people who work inside. When the guards stand on well-lit and comfortable floors, when the docents have broad corridors to guide their tours along, when the education department has space for its films and project rooms, when the board of trustees has a comfortable conference room to meet in, when the museum store has enough shelf space, when the museum café can serve enough people efficiently, then everyone will project the brand of their museum more happily and more effectively. The rumble generated by exciting new architecture is felt deep inside a museum. Realize that your internal workers will be under strain during construction and, depending on the nature of the work, perhaps concerned about new responsibilities to come. Think about specific ways to thank curators, administration, volunteers, store and restaurant personnel, and guards. Give them "building permits," coupons for discounts at the museum store or restaurant, or extra time off. Give a Hard Hat of the Month Award for grace under pressure, or a Builder's Bonus for good ideas that facilitate the construction. This morale boosting makes for good internal branding by keeping your employees updated and enthusiastic about your progressive image.

SIGNATURE DRAWING AND CAMPAIGN SLOGAN

Depending on budget, you may want to mount a special new building advertising campaign, highlighting the energy and look of a construction project. Design an illustration or a symbol that will be the visual signature of the project and use it on all advertising, mailings, signage, and employee memos that you produce. It's relatively inexpensive to create a one-off letterhead that features an illustration of the building, and perhaps a tag line, and write letters to stakeholders to keep them updated. This is also the time to ask for money. New construction of any size is proof of growth and success, and donors like to help those who help themselves.

Everyone is proud to be successful, and new buildings make people proud of their membership in a museum, proud enough to pledge more money. Civic leaders should see your progress as a symbol for the growth of the city itself. Everybody benefits in the wake of a new building, from the local restaurants that feed additional workers, to taxi and bus drivers, to banks and parking meters.

The big brand museum architects have done a service to all museum builders by raising the profiles of museums in general and their popularity in particular. The cult of the architect—and he or she needn't be a star— elevates artists and craftspeople, and demonstrates the power of the individual. Invite the architect or workmen involved in your project to speak to your members and civic leaders about their skills, tools, work schedules, and unique insights and perspectives. Architects and builders, by training, mix creativity and vision with engineering, draftsmanship, technology, management, and a solid work ethic; they're interesting, down-to-earth people who can add new luster to your museum. This new-face factor could be especially memorable for museums that don't rotate their exhibits often, whose name is taken for granted.

PUT THE BUILDING IN PERSPECTIVE

The building or addition might loom large in current day-to-day life, but it's just one aspect of the museum, and it must never overwhelm the institution itself. Select the one photograph of the building that highlights a distinctive feature, and use this shot only. Don't monopolize a brochure with the Building from Every Angle; your marketing piece will look like a baby book. If you create brochures or postcards with images of the new building on the cover, put an artifact on the cover, too. Always remind stakeholders of the whole, not just the new.

One way to put the importance of the building in proportion is to display materials or models of the building in the museum store and restaurant. These will be small models, visually reinforcing that the new addition is just a part of a long and larger tradition. By seeing the models in a familiar place, visitors will connect the new structure with their own experience, rather than as an expensive, perhaps disruptive, change. Humanize the building further by displaying samples of the building materials with a please touch sign. Let visitors feel the museum and the craftsmanship that goes into it.

If your new construction is a gallery or renovation, it's easier to integrate it into the brand of the entire museum. Create and display panels with illustrations of the project, its floor plan, and an architectural detail, and describe the reason for the construction. By showing visitors behind-the-scenes work, they'll understand the museum better and appreciate being informed.

EXPAND YOUR AUDIENCE

A highly visible project, like a new wing or building, interests everybody, even people beyond your usual reach. Smart marketers use "new products," and a new addition qualifies, as an inducement to pull in new audiences. For starters, run ads in nearby city newspapers and radio stations, so you appeal to a wider geographic market. Since your project is news, buy ads in different media than your customary ones, to touch the interests of different demographics and psychographics. Connect with retirement and assisted living centers, where there's a large group of potential members. Your new building may be more accessible to them now. Renew appeals to minority groups. Many minorities don't visit your museum for the sole reason that they haven't been marketed to. Now you have something new to talk about. It's a good occasion to speak more inclusively. Also, a new building might be better located, have more appropriate hours, and more inclusive exhibits. Newness should communicate that there is now a place for them.

Look at typical groups in new categories. Reach out to local colleges, medical centers, and resorts that have transient audiences; now your museum may fit their agenda. Contact elementary teachers at home, not through their schools, and speak to them as individuals rather than caretakers. The construction itself is a subject for adults, and the actual nuts-and-bolts story appeals to people who have interests beyond their job. Notify unions, a group you may not have contact with. You are providing their members with jobs, and that's a door-opener for this excellent target group. Taking their perspective, write press releases, articles, or brochure copy from the point of view of the carpenters and electricians working on the project. Everyone loves being interviewed and it's effective in getting them personally interested in the mission of the museum.

If your new space provides more research capacity, you may find an entire new audience among scholars in your field. Another audience frequently ignored is the one you've lost. There are many reasons, most of them harmless, that visitors stop visiting, and new construction is exciting enough to revive dormant relationships. Customers never really leave good brands; they just wander off in search of something different. Always recontact lapsed members or donors. Another group that fades away is civic leaders and government officials. Many of them just don't get reelected, and the rest return to private life, so remind the group in power of the increased economic and social improvements you're bringing to their community.

Like any marketer, when you have something new and bigger to offer, you can charge more for it. When construction is over, ask for higher levels of giving from existing members, donors, and sponsors. Remember that you're building to better serve your public, and this visible change effects many other changes, in ways both dynamic and memorable.

BRANDING OPS

There are so many opportunities to showcase your brand, all you have to do is keep hammering. From first sketch to last countersinking of the nails, be alert to new ways to tell your constituents about your project and its importance:

- Involve the state and local tourism groups early and often.
- Integrate the architect's thoughts; you'll find that these artists can articulate your image and mission in fresh ways.
- If the new building will be in a new location, send preview maps on postcards to your mailing list.
- Send preview brochures to neighbors in the new location. If you're in a community served by taxis, have a coffee and doughnut party for cabbies.
- Make your new space a part of the community. Invite the local orchestra to perform in the lobby, or the city council to meet there.
- Use street signage for visitors and locals alike—a large surface for displaying the name and logo.
- Commemorate the building whenever possible. The first exhibition will, of course, be tagged the Inaugural Exhibition. This can be repeated the following year with the First Anniversary Exhibition.

University Museums

Children of Strong Parents

Museums under the aegis of colleges and universities, foundations or corporations risk losing their identity to that of the generous parent. They may or may not owe their building, curators, access, name, and very existence to the larger entity; they may or may not share control in mounting effective exhibitions, assembling boards, collecting donations, renting out their facilities, or providing a museum store or café. Most likely filial museums engage in ongoing negotiations between autonomy and largesse, and their brand is, therefore, vulnerable. It's in the interest of both parent and child that the museum maintains its identity and brand.

The need for branding is as strong for the associated museum as it is for the independent ones. They need to create an identity separate from the redoubtable personality of the academy. They need to establish their credentials in the museum community and, even harder, in the wider community where up to now they've been overshadowed by the dominant personality. They need a defined mission that might be at odds with the encyclopedic offerings of a university, or the market-driven goals of a corporation. It is especially important to have a distinct image since it's logical for all stakeholders to assume that the parent is supplying and informing everything.

Some of the branding issues are unique to a university-connected museum. In this case branding is essential to create for visitors a picture of a pleasant one-hour museum visit, not a four-year education. Clear-cut branding illuminates for donors the institution they are contributing to.

Museum employees need to understand that the nature of museums is service, not quite the introspection of a research lab or library. Prospective volunteers need to be reassured that this is a place for people with curiosity, not only those with exalted degrees. With a distinct identity, the college museum can announce to the museum universe that it observes the guidelines to interpret, as well as collect and preserve. It will be better equipped to define to scholars its specific area of scholarship.

To the wider world beyond the campus, the museum must communicate that it has wide open galleries, not hidden stacks and carrels. It will inform elementary school educators whether its exhibits are open to schoolchildren and not just undergrads. In many ways, and regularly, it will remind local governments and media of its separate existence and purpose. Gown continues to live apart from town, and that presents museums with the opportunity to build bridges to the advantage of both sides.

Because an umbrella entity confers many advantages, not limited to financial support, automatic awareness, and prestige, college and university museums, as well as corporate museums, will want to salute their parent while maintaining their individual identity. There are many ways they can burnish their own image while still benefiting from the halo effect of the other.

KEEPING A PROUD CONSISTENCY

Although all museums observe the branding basics of a consistent look, typeface, color palette, tag line, message, and tone of voice, it is more important when another, better-known brand shares the page. Small brands appear bigger when they speak consistently. As noted ealier, all materials—from letterhead and business cards to brochures, signs, and Web site—should have the same look. A prominent logo cuts through a lot of competition, and it doesn't have to be big or in color. It goes without saying that the logo should be used consistently, all the time. One way to check if the mark or typeface is distinctive in a clutter is to see how readable it is when reduced, photocopied several times, or sent by fax. When the logo appears with the university, corporate, or foundation logo, it will hold its own if placed higher up on the page, or if it's surrounded by white space. Perhaps the museum logo can be in color, and the parent logo in black and white. Another way to stand out is to appear in multiple places, on the front and back of a brochure, for example, or as a design element throughout a marketing piece. All this is negotiable, and the design department can be a formidable ally in proving to the parent that the museum's prominence in no way outshines the parent's.

An overall signature color helps establish an identity for the museum, regardless how visible the parent logo. Picture a museum where all the signs, wall labels, brochures, visitor tags, employee badges, and store shopping bags are printed on color stock. That's a strong identity that allows the parent organization to place its name on every page.

With all the space on a Web site—unlimited pages and endless scrolls—there is a temptation to include the parent everywhere. It's like the kids having such a big house, Mom and Dad can move in almost unnoticed. It doesn't work in real life or in museum branding. On a Web site, where the images pop on fast and lively, every mention of the parent organization steals energy from the offshoot museum. One prestigious university has its name and seal on every page of its equally prestigious museum's site. It communicates the stability and omnipresence of the university, rather than the excitement and discovery of the museum. A well-designed Web site with a distinctive look will retain the solidity of the former plus the exploration of the latter. Use the museum's (not the school's) colors throughout. Put the museum tag line or mission statement on every page. Deploy as visuals the artifacts that are a museum's stock in trade. Use sound, a subtle and powerful enhancer of image. In any response devices or name-gathering techniques, direct inquiries to the museum's address. And while you're using these interactive features of the Web, add some entertainment with interactive questions or games that illustrate the museum's holdings. If the museum has a store, hype it—merchandise clearly says "museum."

VISITOR EXPERIENCE

Museums that are situated on a campus, rather than a city street or even a cultural park, start the visitor experience poorly. Too many university museums look like classroom buildings, and from the outset, visiting a campus museum is confusing. Directional signs are needed to show the way, all the way up to the front door. And the confusion doesn't end there. The entrances are cold and empty, sometimes with no information desk, or one that looks like an afterthought. In a university building, of course, most people know where they are going. In a museum, most people don't, and signs are needed to dispel the strangeness and intimidation. If your building looks like somebody else's dormitory instead of looking inviting, and you can't call an architect, there are some changes you can implement immediately.

Inside the museum, blazon the name or logo on every sign, wall label, and panel. These are constant reminders to visitors that they are in the museum, not the university. Mount video screens with a docent giving information or curators working on an exhibit, some activity to add liveliness to a place that frequently has none. Part of the lack of life in a college, or corporate, museum is lack of staff. If you do staff the museum, supply all docents, guards, museum store assistants, and information desk personnel with badges and name tags that bear the museum's name and logo. Since college faculty and researchers move through the galleries, their IDs would benefit from the same museum graphics.

The lobby is supposed to be a staging area, where visitors acclimate to the experience ahead. This sometimes seems like a luxury in an academic environment, but there are academic ways to make the entrance more welcoming. Provide an information desk, not a guard station, and stock it with informative—and well-branded—brochures.

In addition to staff, build a few high-impact displays that quickly communicate your mission. Supply a small store with educational items that reinforce your mission. Furnish the lobby with chairs or banquettes, so visitors can relax and reflect as they would in a stand-alone museum, and then provide visuals to give them more to reflect on. Posters on the wall are inexpensive ways to build in a contemporary look, and also seed some ideas.

NOT A REAL MUSEUM

University museums have an advantage that other museums don't: they don't have to educate the public about the advantages of museum-going. They just have to tell the museum-going public that they exist. On the other hand, university museums are perceived by the public as not being "real" museums. When prospective visitors think the campus museum isn't authentic, it's a big problem just begging for the skills of branding. Branding is all about mission and identity, and how to communicate the core values of your museum clearly. Branding doesn't so much sell a museum, as define it.

When a Midwest university museum conducted consumer research, it discovered that nonvisitors thought its collections consisted only of student and faculty art, that they didn't have "real" art in their holdings. Although three galleries were devoted to the permanent collection, and a ground-floor gallery displayed European art, no one knew. The staff was so accustomed to their space that they never looked through the eyes of the public. Another precept of branding: it's not what you say but what the consumer perceives. With this branding insight, it pays to conduct focus groups to see how to appeal to the people who know the university but not the museum. Any marketing professor can help design research.

In distinguishing the museum from the school, a few "town" techniques will work very well. Some colleges publish newsletters that feature a Curator Column to a different work from the permanent collection. The newsletter can carry the tag line that defines the museum's distinct personality, and it can run stories and photos that show real people enjoying the real museum. Campus newsletters have a built-in mailing list that can be inexpensively expanded to include the town's ZIP codes, businesses, and other community organizations.

Another university initiative sent anonymous employees, the equivalent of buzz marketers, into the streets of town, posing as visiting conference attendees looking for the "conference site" at the museum.

Predictably, museums surrounded by students discovered that that segment of the local market wanted rock bands, a place to meet friends, and beverages. Though most museums can't offer anything more stimulating than coffee, a real problem is that student leisure time doesn't usually start at 6:00 p.m. Museums appealing to adults do very well with free lectures and open houses.

Some of the other branding conflicts between a museum and its parent are as minor as a two-part, unwieldy name, and as major as the differing attitudes toward planning. Curators are trained to be scholars, not marketers, and in a college environment it's easy to look inward instead of outward toward the museum visitor. Corporations rush effortlessly into marketing, with less attention to the overview of the museum collection. Again, branding guides the museum administration through the steps to success: clear definition of mission, presentation of a consistent brand image, and a system for discovering visitor perception. With a strong brand, what naturally follows is a focused giving plan, a template for thought-provoking exhibitions, and a broadening of education. A significant by-product is independence.

Future Members

Identifying with College Students

If ever a museum needed a strong brand image, it's when trying to identify with college students. Ten years after the field trip, these young adults still carry the memories—smiles and tears—from their first visits. Exploration, discovery, freedom—children of all ages uncover magic in museums and remember specifics for years. They connect indelible memories with a name and place and carry brand names in their hearts for life.

In capturing the youth market, remember that young people come in three distinct age groups, each with different learning and enjoyment needs. Elementary school children are well served by school trips and parents. Twenty-somethings enjoy companionship with their culture, and discover museums through evening events and their own growing awareness of enrichment. College students, the most obvious target for exploration and new learning, are the hardest to reach. The steady call of coursework, part-time jobs, bottomless need for sleep, and heightened sociability combines to shove museum-going off their radar. We'll spend most of this chapter on college students. To know where young people are coming from, it helps to see museums as they saw them as children.

TOO MUCH HERDING, TOO FEW SEATS

Research reveals a few bad memories for young people can arise from several sources: some stemming from early field trips when they felt corralled and herded, when adults stared at them for being rambunctious, and when they were forbidden to explore. A large proportion of today's young people remember disliking the lack of comfort in a museum; they found them too cold or too hot, crowded, noisy, and without a place to sit. They got hungry. They felt out of control and didn't know where they were going next. Children carry long memories of museum security personnel who were seen as guarding them, not the artifacts. Young adults tell researchers that they remember being hassled and suspected, or stared at for being noisy. Early on they got a message that museums were not for exploration, not for sharing experiences. On the other hand, there was a suggestion in focus groups with college students that museums sometimes evoke feelings of self-awareness. Along with freedom to talk, it seems that museum field trips also need to provide young people with space to be alone.

In addition to the memories of early field trips, college students also remember the rigorous not-for-profit project required of them in high school. Though not all are burned by the former, many are burned out by the latter. Museums are just another cultural amenity they can gladly forgo until graduation.

AWE AND RESPECT

On the positive side, college students really love museums. In-depth discussions in focus groups revealed that many actually have been to a museum in the last year, and most enjoyed the trip. They assume their friends don't visit museums, until follow-up research showed that most of them do. Many go with boyfriends or girlfriends, and seem as proud of the attachment as the museum visit. Surprisingly, many college students still visit museums with their parents or grandparents, perhaps on family trips.

Based on discussions with college students, there are several actions museums can take to heighten their brand and image with college students.

Since collegiality is a near-universal trait, college students visit museums with friends, and like to talk and giggle once they get there. They feel frustrated when they can't share the museum experience. Brands are built when people agree about the distinctiveness and worthiness of a product. Museums also need spaces or systems for talking out loud and comparing notes.

College students need to know exactly what to look for, and why it's important. Museums would do well to list their offerings clearly, state why they're significant, and supplement the concept with plenty of coherent signs and labels, if not study guides. Students buy books at the museum store, clearly appreciating the education aspect of museums. Signage that ties the merchandise to the exhibit can reinforce the visit and the museum brand. Because of their close relationship with knowledge, students notice the lack of it; after all, they're skilled at critiquing their professors. Some of them notice that the guards, staff, and volunteers aren't knowledgeable, and seem not to care about the exhibits that surround them. Students characterize these employees as not cultured and less than admirable aspects of the museum. Good branding includes training the employees who represent the museum to the public face to face.

Despite the fact that college students are part of an intellectual cohort, many think that museums are snobbish and elite, that they only cater to the "Upper Class." Branding has gone dangerously wrong here and all museums share the burden of reversing this opinion. It will start with attitudes fostered in elementary school field trips, and continue with every touchpoint mentioned in the preceding chapters. Brands that eschew elitism will live and breathe non-elitism. One laudatory example is Chicago's Museum of Contemporary Art, which does a prodigious job of user-friendliness, starting with the water bowl for dogs on its front steps, the college-age men and women who staff the lobby desk, and the not-so-fearsome guards who wear T-shirts with "Fear No Art" printed on them.

More serious is the probability that one group of college students— those from low economic backgrounds—haven't been marketed to at all. Research revealed that African-American students never receive mailings to their ZIP codes, never see ads on buses that travel through their neighborhoods, never hear PSA announcements on the radio stations they enjoy. It's essential that museums reexamine their marketing strategies and make sure they reach underserved communities.

Despite the elitism and inaccessibility that some young people perceive, most see status and they like it. They like being part of a prestigious museum. Some even complain that other visitors don't dress very well for such an occasion. They feel pride in being at a learning place, in pushing themselves to a higher level; this is intellectual mobility, a very desirable social climbing. Wherever your brand touches the college student, make it synonymous with learning. Consider offering erudite books at prices college students can afford. Make an effort to identify college students when they visit independently and get their college contact information. This not only associates you with their life, but collects data for further undergraduate relationships.

IF YOU LOVE MUSEUMS, LOVE MY MUSEUM

With the right product and promotions, college students will embrace museums, and the next step is for them to engage in your museum, not just the generic experience. This is not territoriality, but building. Museums need young, energetic members who will be advocates, and advocacy stems from involvement with a mission. Students want to be involved, to belong, and to work hard on a vision they respect. College-level reading materials, available at the exhibits (and well-branded, of course), reinforce the brand in a manner meaningful to students. Museums that have performance space should brand them loud and strong; these are college student magnets. And since the goal of attracting college students is not just education, but membership, design strong development programs beamed specifically to them.

STUDENTS OF THE WORLD

Staking out your museum's place in the world resonates with college students who are just discovering the world. This is the age when they travel overseas, study abroad, and meet foreign students at their own colleges. Museums in foreign places have a cachet with college students that American museums can co-opt. College students today are not only aware of cultural differences and very accepting of them, they like them. They see internationalism as a status symbol. Multiculturalism is a core requirement in many colleges. Wherever your museum intersects with the world, in collections, exhibitions, personnel, or architecture, flaunt it. Being a part of the world will enrich your brand and make it meaningful to our new global citizens.

GO TO COLLEGE

All traits of college students point to one common denominator: their college. This is the very specific place where they invest most of their time, money, and energy. Even students with part-time jobs now talk about putting education first. Colleges and universities build so many clubs, internships, and creative projects into the curriculum that they truly rule. Museums need the membership potential of students, and they also benefit from the systems of today's colleges. Happily, any size or genre of museum can play.

Internships are becoming the sine qua non of student resumes, and museums need help. It takes only a little preparation to turn your non-paying job into a valid internship. Most colleges have internship coordinators or career offices that pair prospective interns with prospective employers. The museum agrees to give and supervise meaningful tasks. The college agrees to grant credit for the experience. Part of your promise is to instill your museum's core values to the student working for you. With the student intern also comes the administrator on campus, the student's adviser and teachers, friends, and classmates. Each internship brings a wide circle of college contacts.

Internships often lead to jobs and an ongoing relationship with the internship director. Being part of the curriculum ensures a relationship with the college. More and more schools are developing museum studies programs, and they look to local museums to round out the curriculum. In other words, along with courses in management, education, history of art, or display design, there will be a course titled "Internship." As part of the curriculum, a museum becomes a regular name in the catalog, a teacher on the adjunct roster, and a course developer with the department chair. It's a high-profile position. For any community with several museums and a college, especially smaller communities, it's a fine way to train a new generation of museum professionals.

New programs of study don't get proposed every year, but guest lecturers are always needed, and museums have many experts who could lend new insights to an art, history, science, or humanities class. Guest lectures usually last an hour, so the time commitment is reasonable. Most talks these days include a PowerPoint visual component, and that does take preparation. A corollary is to hold the guest lecture, in the form of a field trip, at the museum.

An exciting new area of museum-university collaboration is epitomized by the medical school course that sends its students to art museums to diagnose the people in the pictures. The course developers say it is excellent medical training, in the best tradition of humanistic science. Planetariums have always been used to teach astronomy, natural history museums to objectify anthropology. Now there's a way to spread the reach of any museums. Marketing students can follow the lead of the med students, and categorize those portraits into market segments. Interior Design students will visit house museums to see period furnishings. Math students will visit those science museums to calculate canoe speed, or size of planets. Colleges want to fortify critical-thinking skills, and they are looking for new teaching techniques. Museums have the wherewithal to be valuable allies.

As museums brainstorm ideas for programs or lecturers, they target a whole different segment by factoring in college students and the curricula at local colleges, a prospect pool that includes teachers and administrators. Another way to develop programs and market them at the same time: put together focus groups of students that probe their interests. Like all research, with every bit of information that comes in to the museum, information on the museum flows out to the marketplace. In lieu of focus groups, questionnaires might be sent to selected college classes, or even orientation sessions. College student affairs offices are looking for ways to involve students in the culture of the community. For students who are already inside the museum, an interactive computer in the lobby is a higher-tech way to garnish information, and the data might prove richer. In the environment of the Internet, many questions can be asked, and where college students might balk at filling out comment cards, they attack the keyboard with fingers flying. One big question to be answered concerns advertising media. It's essential to know what radio stations students listen to, what they read, where they see out of home advertising. School newspapers and bulletin boards continue to be the best way to reach students. Buzz marketing, the au courant term for what used to be called word of mouth or the student grapevine, is another, though less reliable, possibility.

One overlooked medium is starting to get attention: church. For African-American students, especially, a significant amount of information is transmitted at church. Whereas students pay only sporadic attention to newspapers, radio, and even the Internet, they engage meaningfully with their church, and give enormous credence to ministers and fellow parishioners. In fact many of the guest lectures, off-site or on, that are developed for colleges can be repurposed for church groups. To widen the window even more, contact other college-age organizations such as international students or curriculum-based clubs. Youth who already donate their time are the kind of dedicated people you want to nurture to membership. They all are looking for relevant programs, and with a little thinking you can relate your brand to their interests.

The need to belong is strong with college students, many of whom are away from home, all of whom are going through the separation from parent process. An invitation to become a guest curator will give many students with good ideas a place to apply them. Their ideas keep you abreast of their interests, something that even the most sophisticated corporate marketers have trouble discerning. In fact, you could probably interest corporate sponsors to partner in this endeavor. Although you would identify students through their schools, or church, this would be a museum-to-individual activity, with many advantages. You'll alert young people to careers in museums, energize their community, and develop a broader audience. It's quite possible you'll get media attention, for this is not only an activity that highlights your image, but a model for many not-for-profits.

Community service combined with class work, or service learning, is gaining favor at many colleges, and they need viable programs to partner with. Unlike an internship, these programs are structured through the classes, so museums wouldn't reap as many student-hours as they would with an intern. However, they gain the semester-long support of the class instructor, and a closer relationship with the school itself. It's another way to align your name with the service-oriented students. Partnerships, like internships, exact extra time for supervision, and small museums might not have the time. Sometimes they just need extra hands for heavy lifting. Big jobs are no problem for young people, and some of the projects you've put on the back burner can be given to them. These are jobs like cleaning storage areas, laying sod, and moving furniture to new quarters. They may not seem "museum quality" to you, but they are fun ways for groups of young people to get to know the museum up close and personally, even before they're involved with its contents. Call it pre-branding, it's an excellent on-ramp for future members.

After the recruiting comes the retention. It's the number one goal of colleges, keeping students semester after semester, and it's the museum's goal as well. These are the next generation of members and supporters and they must keep coming back. A good brand facilitates retention; it feels like home and its stakeholders want to come back. First, make students feel at home. Give them a museum membership card or, if they're doing a job, a name tag. If you're giving a guest lecture in the classroom, take a few minutes to define the goals of the museum and its place in the community. Where appropriate, describe the students' role in the mission. When students are working at the museum, take publicity photos and send them to hometown newspapers. At any meeting with students, distribute material and, a more adult gesture, business cards. College students are no longer just field trippers but part of the process, so keep them in the fold with newsletters and follow-up mailings, preferably to e-mail addresses, which last longer and have a built-in "address change requested." Some museum administrators wonder about the long-term advantage of a college student, who change addresses about every nine months. It is true that some of the retention will benefit a museum in another city. However, maintaining undergraduate interest will always be worthwhile.

Keep your name on campus with regular announcements posted on bulletin boards, and internship opportunities posted on college job sites. After guest lectures, or work projects, hand out bring-a-friend tickets or coupons for specially marked museum store merchandise. Whether the activity is on site or on campus, have a sign-in sheet (on letterhead, of course). Once you've attracted college students, don't let them get away, because they'll be card-carrying adults very soon.

College students are not a stand-alone segment. They come attached, firmly, to their college, institutions museums should also stay attached to. Keep administrators updated on your internships, jobs, and programs. Supply them with posters and brochures. To capture more attention, and at a higher level, offer pieces from your collection to embellish the décor of administrative offices or public spaces. Label these exhibits with the museum logo and Web site address, plus enough information to give the flavor of the whole museum.

Sponsor a club competition, or the debate team. Usually it's a business that brands itself through sponsorships, but depending on your focus, it could be a noteworthy match-up. Your logo on a team T-shirt or booth is buzz advertising at its best, and you could be the first museum to utilize this new form of nontraditional marketing.

■ ■ ■

College students respect museums and feel pride in getting involved. They appreciate the business of museums, and the details that go into running them. To discover new activities that their parents haven't already found is empowering, and their potency is something to harness. At college age, young people tend to be brand loyal and it behooves all museums to reach out to them with offers of a comfortable place to expend their substantial energy and intelligence.

Epilogue

Going Forward

With branding in place, a museum is ready for anything. Every opportunity, every dilemma, unfolds more easily when a museum understands its identity and core values. By the mere act of addressing the brand issues, museums and their people make progress.

The goal of "museum branding" is to emphasize the far-ranging power of a brand and how it is reflected at every touchpoint, from exhibition to Web site, from the board of trustees to the volunteer tour guide, from development to education. "Museum branding" provides the vocabulary for assessing any situation and teaches museum professionals to deliberate: Is this event consistent with our brand image? How does our store merchandise reinforce our mission? Does the staff buy in to our core values? Is this solicitation letter on brand? Every activity or operation can be considered part of the brand, so it's necessary to conduct regular brand audits to constantly check that the message is consistent and that the image is clear. Branding keeps a museum on track with all its constituents.

But where is the track leading? The world now demands more of museums, and going forward is where branding proves its importance.

The challenges come from four places: the not-for-profit universe with its many competitors; the wider and pervasive world of business, whose successes and faults inform the not-for-profit sector; the community, which desires our involvement; and museums themselves, to improve upon what is already excellent.

FIRST, THE NOT-FOR-PROFIT UNIVERSE

In competing with other arts and culture entities for the not-for-profit dollar, a well-branded museum is well prepared. Museums already understand and implement relationship marketing, the essential ingredient of developing a base of supporters. No other not-for-profit category relates so well.

Building enduring relationships has been a tenet of for-profit marketers for years. Ironically, this people principle has been underutilized by the culture people. It's not enough to sell memberships, season tickets, or promotional offers to lock in support; these are good-enough systems that museums, symphonies, and theater companies have been doing for a long time. The challenge is to better understand the market segments and life stages of your individual supporters, and communicate with them individually. Museums have delved deeply into the lives of their constituents and the good brands will keep them loyal. The management of data, made easier and infinitely more sophisticated by the computer, has already resulted in lists that can be segmented dozens of ways. What breathes life into these activities is the trust that names on a list give a good brand, and the respect that museums give back. Building an enduring relationship with the visitor you already have is easy with a consistent branding program. Branding reminds recipients of what they like best about you and reinforces it. The steady reinforcement of core values results in trust that can last a lifetime and a relationship that grows and changes with the times.

The notion of customer lifetime value is fairly new. It's not easy to envision, let alone implement, retaining a customer from fourth-grade field trip to will. Yet, as supporters age, move, and assume new responsibilities, they need never distance themselves from the museum they love. Their interests evolve from onlooker to donor to advocate, and it's up to museums to nurture this evolution. Importantly, many brand loyalists deed this attitude to their children, keeping their favorite arts organization in the family across the generations.

Museums are particularly suited to maintaining vitality across time and space. Each museum brand tells a unique story, rich in narrative and bolstered with visuals. With the interactivity of Web sites, tangibility of museum stores, and accessibility of exhibitions, every supporter can be retained.

SECOND, THE BUSINESS MODEL

As for the business of museums, business has never been tougher. The skills brought by strong financial, legal, and marketing managers will, in the coming years, be tested by the twin challenges of transparency and accountability. What Sarbanes-Oxley imposed on corporate America, the donor advocacy groups are demanding for not-for-profits. Museums are already highly visible and accountable. They will be more so.

Here again, a strong brand is a strong ally. A museum's mission is clear for all to see when branding is in place. Good branding demands consistency of every message, at every touchpoint, to every constituent. This is easier said than done, and it requires that the brand identity be revisited regularly, and that brand audits be conducted. Then, every acquisition, every solicitation, every hire will be aware of the museum's core values.

On a practical level, branding saves money. Printed materials carry more impact, donor calls needn't be repeated as often, board members understand the value of their financial commitment; the list of economies goes on and on.

One business trend sheds a brilliant light on museums: corporate social responsibility (CSR). Social consciousness is nothing new in corporate America, but for years it has been the job of nonline staffers, community relations departments, or human resource folks. Responsibility with a capital "R" is a new species of proactiveness, blessed from the top of the reporting chain and frequently initiated by the CEO. Companies with CSR lead and innovate, and they love partnering with not-for-profit organizations that have a distinctive brand identity. In addition to museums' halo effect, business likes museums' track record of education, culture, and community involvement. It doesn't hurt if they also have a good mailing list and are housed in interesting facilities. There's more to CSR than just mutually beneficial cause marketing. The partnership is long-lasting, beyond promotional spikes.

Though the future can be forecast with multisyllable concepts like relationship marketing, customer lifetime value, accountability, transparency, and corporate social responsibility, it can also be defined by one deceptively small word: change.

THREE, COMMUNITY INVOLVEMENT

Change is the trend that everyone fears. Things change and existing ideas and systems lose currency. It's happening in every aspect of our multicultured society and communities are racing to keep up. Strong brands make change less scary because their mission and core values carry on. Robust brands don't just cope with change, they relish it.

Museums with a strong sense of self are poised to shoulder the culture changes that flummox our communities. From homeschooling to stretched workdays to terrorism, those who care look to those who can. And if terrorism seems a little global for the local museum, remember that after September 11, 2001, museums saw an increase in visitors who, the conventional wisdom goes, were looking for a place of stability and honor, if only for a little while.

You needn't look far to find a museum with a day care program, English as a second language class, or teacher certification program. It's not a stretch to envision GED courses, town hall meetings, and creative financing for local projects. Creativity knows no bounds in museums, and the good brands can generate that energy outward, as well as internally.

FOUR, CHANGE THYSELF

"We used to say," an astute marketing professional claimed, "'if it ain't broke, don't fix it.' Now we say, 'if it ain't broke, break it.'"

Museums also have their marching orders to break with tradition whenever feasible. This does not mean breaking rules or breaking hearts. It means esteeming the robustness of change and the many benefits thereof. One sees change all the time in exciting exhibitions, ambitious buildings, and new faces in the galleries. Even the categorization of museums is changing, as art museums embrace science, history museums address current issues, and presidential museums get lively. Very few cultural institutions can meet the challenges of a multicultural world as multiexperientially as museums can.

■　■　■

Nobody tells a story like museums can. When it comes to communicating to the world, and mediating messages between different worlds, museums rule. A respected brand with a distinct image and beloved personality can carry the discourse forward all the way.

References

BOOKS, JOURNALS, AND NEWSPAPERS

Adams, Steve. "The Brander's Guide to the Galaxy." *SAM* 2 (November/December 2001): 29–30.

Barnes, Julian E. "Cloning Colonial Williamsburg." *New York Times* (13 June 2001): sec. C.

"Berkshire Hathaway Inc. Official Home Page." www.berkshirehathaway.com.

Blake, Kathy. "Boston's Museum of Fine Arts Initiating Major Renovation Effort." *Nation's Restaurant News* 31 (5 May 1997): 72.

Brech, Poppy. "Guardian Newspapers Sponsor the Tate." *Marketing* (16 March 2000): 8e.

Brenson, Michael. *Visionaries and Outcasts: The NEA, Congress, and the Place of the Visual Artist in America.* New York: The New Press, 2001.

"The Case for Brands." *Economist* 360 (6 September 2001): 11.

"A Cautionary Tale." *Art Monthly* 230 (October 1999): 20.

Chew, Ron. "In Praise of the Small Museum." *Museum News* 81 (March/April 2002): 36–41.

Ciccotti, Susan. "Curator of the Stars." *Museum News* 79 (May/June 2000): 11–13.

———. "New Approach to the Old Conundrum." *Museum News* 79 (July/August 2000): 11–13.

Conn, Steven, Ivan Karp, and Kimberly Rorshach. "Museums in Public Life." *Odyssey,* broadcast on WBEZ–Chicago Public Radio, 28 January 2002.

Cristol, Steven M. and Peter Sealey. *Simplicity Marketing: End Brand Complexity, Clutter, and Confusion.* New York: The Free Press, 2000.

Cross, K. Patricia and Mimi Harris Steadman. *Classroom Research: Implementing the Scholarship of Teaching.* San Francisco: Jossey-Bass, 1996.

Cuno, James, ed. *Whose Muse? Art Museums and the Public Trust.* Cambridge, MA: Princeton University Press, 2004.

Defty, Sally. "Hubbub over Zigzag." *Art News* 100 (June 2001): 67.

Donlon, J. P. "Zen and the Art of Cause-Related Marketing." *Chief Executive* 138 (October 1998): 51–57.

Eakin, Blake. "The Incredible Growing Art Museum." *Art News* 100 (October 2001): 138–49.

Falk, John H. and Lynn D. Dierking. "School Field Trips: Assessing Their Long-Term Impact." *Curator* 40 (September 1997): 211–18.

Filler, Martin. "The Museum Game: The Guggenheim Wants to Recreate Bilbao on Wall Street." *New Yorker* (17 April 2000).

Finke, Gail Deibler. "Brand Awareness: Museum Style." *Visual Merchandising and Store Design* 127 (October 1996): 138–42.

Forgey, Benjamin. "The MoMA Track: Museum Sets Up Shop in Queens." *Washington Post* (23 June 2002): sec. G.

"Forty Action Strategies." *The NASAA Advocate* 5 no. 4 (2000).

Friedman, Thomas L. *The Lexus and the Olive Tree*. New York: Farrar, Straus and Giroux, 1999.

"From Sales to Branding." *Just an Online Minute*. www.mediapost.com. 18 December 2000.

Gaia, Giuliano. "Promoting a Museum Website on the Net." Paper presented at the Museums and the Web Conference, New Orleans, Louisiana, 12–14 March 2000.

Gates, Christopher T. "Forum: Democracy & the Civic Museum." *Museum News* 80 (May/June 2001): 47–55.

"Glass: The Corning Museum of Glass." *@issue* 6, no. 1 (2000): 6–13.

Gopnik, Adam. "Books: The Habit of Democracy: Alexis de Tocqueville and the Pleasures of Citizenship." *New Yorker* (15 October 2001): 212–16.

Gronlund, M., A. Weinberg, and A. Yang. "Tracking the Building Boom." *Art News* 100 (October 2001): 142–45.

Gurian, Elaine Heumann. Paper presented at the American Association of Museums Annual Conference, Dallas, Texas, 11–15 May 2002.

Hacker, Robert C. "The End of Brand Marketing on the Web?" *Target Marketing* 23 (January 2000): 42–44.

Harris, Neil. "The Divided House of the American Art Museum." *Daedalus* 128 (Summer 1999): 33–56.

Harvey, Mark L., Ross J. Loomis, Paul A. Bell, and Margaret Marino. "The Influence of Museum Exhibit Design on Immersion and Psychological Flow." *Environment and Behavior* 30 (September 1998): 60.

Hass, Kristin Ann. "The Knowledge Producers." Review of *Museums and American Intellectual Life, 1876–1926*, by Steven Conn. *Museum News* 80 (September/October 2001): 22–25.

Heller, Scott. "Treasure-House? Creative Laboratory? Hi-Tech Cultural Center? What Will the Art Museum of the 21st Century Be?" *Art News* 96 (November 1997): 96–99.

Hoeller, A. Hildegard. "Monument to the Consuming Self: Isabella Stewart Gardner Museum." Paper presented at the American Culture Association, Philadelphia, Pennsylvania, April 2001.

Holt, Nancy. "Milwaukee Pulls Out Stops in Museum Project." *Wall Street Journal* (14 February 2001): sec. B.

Iovine, Julie V. "Whitney Museum Biennial Invites Architecture In." *New York Times* (21 February 2002): sec. B.

Jones, Chris. "The Corporate Seduction of Museums." *Chicago Tribune* (16 January 2003): sec. 7.

Kahn, Douglas. *Noise, Water, Meat: A History of Sound in the Arts*. Cambridge, MA: The MIT Press, 1999.

Kinzer, Stephen. "Many State Arts Councils Make Their Case and Survive Budget Cuts." *New York Times* (8 January 2004): sec. E.

Kirsner, Scott. "Branding Tall." *CIO* 12 (1 December 1998): 298–30.

Klein, Naomi. *No Logo: Taking Aim at Brand Bullies*. New York: Picador, 2000.

Kotler, Neil and Philip Kotler. *Museum Strategy and Marketing: Designing Missions, Building Audiences, Generating Revenue and Resources*. San Francisco: Jossey-Bass, 1998.

Kramer, Louise. "Putting More Store in Commercial Efforts: Cultural Groups Add Income with Gift Shops, Web Sites, Other Ventures." *Crain's New York Business* 16 (27 March 2000): 39.

Larson, Jan. "The Museum Is Open." *American Demographics* 11 (1994): 32–36.

Lavin, Maur. "Who Gets to Say What to Whom?" *Inform* 13 no. 2 (2001): 13–15.

Lavine, Steven and Ivan Karp, eds. *Exhibiting Culture: The Poetics and Politics of Museum Display*. Washington, D.C.: Smithsonian Institution Press, 1991.

Letts, Christine W., William P. Ryan, and Allen Grossman. *High Performance Nonprofit Organizations: Managing Upstream for Greater Impact*. New York: John Wiley & Sons, 1999.

Levy, Paul. "The Hermitage Moves West, Extending the Brand." *Wall Street Journal* (4 January 2002): sec. A.

Lewis, Michael. "Building with Attitude: The 'Look at Me' Strut of a Swagger Building." *New York Times* (6 January 2002): sec. 4.

"Look Out: Ideas & Trends on the Horizon for Creative Professionals." *Graphic Design USA* 36 (June 2000): 5.

Maehara, Paulette V. "Giving in America: 6 New Trends in Fund Raising." *Museum News* 82 (March/April 2003): 35–37, 62–65.

Mand, Adrienne. "Anatomy of a Branding Device: Branding Benchmark." *Mediaweek* 9 (15 March 1999): 142–145.

McPherson, Michael. Review of *Emotional Branding: The New Paradigm for Connecting Brands to People*, by Marc Gobe. *Design Management Journal* 12 (Fall 2001).

"Mississippi Arts Pavilion, Jackson, MI." *New York Times* (3 June 2001): Travel.

Muchnic, Suzanne. "National News: Koolhaas's Big Tent." *Art News* 101 (February 2002): 56.

Muschamp, Herbert. "Architecture Review: Frank Gehry's Vision of Renovating Democracy." *New York Times* (18 May 2001): Arts.

———. "Imaginative Leaps into the Real World." *New York Times* (25 February 2001): Arts.

———. "A Poet's Bridge, Pedestrian Only in Function." *New York Times* (9 September 2001): Arts.

———. "A Rare Opportunity for Real Architecture." *New York Times* (23 October 2000): sec. 2.

———. "When Getting to It Is Part of a Museum's Aesthetic." *New York Times* (26 November 2000): Arts.

Nagai, Asami. "Changing the Face of Public Museums." *Daily Yomiuri* (7 February 2002).

"Niche Widens for Museum Shops." *Chain Store Age* 76 (1 March 2000): 180–2.

Nichols, Judith E. "Pinpointing Affluence." *Fund Raising Management* 25 (May 1994): 13–15.

Reda, Susan. "Museums Find Treasure in Booming Retail Business." *Store* 10 (1997): 70–74.

Reilly, Bernard F., Jr. "Merging or Diverging? New International Business Models from the Web." *Museum News* 80 (January/February 2001): 48–55, 84, 86.

Roberts, Kevin. "Brand Identity 2000: Redefining the World." *Advertising Age* 49 (29 November 1999): 50.

Scott, A. O. "The Year in Ideas: Beauty Is Back." *New York Times* (9 December 2001).

Serrell, Beverly. *Exhibit Labels: An Interpretive Approach.* Walnut Creek, CA: AltaMira Press, 1996.

———. "Paying Attention: The Duration and Allocation of Visitors' Time in Museum Exhibitions." *Curator* 40 (April 1997): 108–13.

Shapiro, Michael. "Museums On-Line Workshop." Presented at the World Intellectual Property Organization Conference on Electronic Commerce and Intellectual Property, 1999.

Sheridan, Margaret. "Turn Right at the Ruby Slippers." *Restaurants & Institutions* 110 (1 August 2000): 91–96.

Smallwood, Lola. "The Wooing of Boeing: Arts Groups Join the Slow Dance." *Chicago Tribune* (25 May 2001).

Solomon, Deborah. "The Year in Ideas: Forget the Art—It's All about the Building." *New York Times Magazine* (9 December 2001): 73.

Szántó, András. "The Business of Art." *American Prospect* 11 (28 February 2000): 39–41.

"Tate Rebranding Urges 'Look Again, Think Again.'" *Graphic Design USA* 36 (July 2000): 19.

"UBIT and Gift Tax Defined for Two Museums." *Aviso* (July 2002): 5.

Van Den Broek, Astrid. "Beyond Banners: Brand Icons and Logos Are on Exhibit as Museums and Galleries Warm Up to the Idea of More-Involved Corporate Sponsorships." *Marketing Magazine* 104, 42 (1999): 22.

Vogel, Carol. "More Growth for Guggenheim." *New York Times* (1 June 2001): sec. B.

———. "Sotheby's Finds Room for Fun." *New York Times* (15 June 2001): sec. B.

Volkert, James W. "Creative Writings." Review of *Interactive Excellence: Defining and Developing New Standards for the Twenty-first Century*, by Edwin Schlossberg. *Museum News* 80 (March/April 2001): 25–29.

Walkup, Carolyn. "Art Museums Sculpt Profits from New Medium: Foodservice." *Nation's Restaurant News* 30 (8 January 1996): 7.

"Who's Wearing the Trousers?" *Economist* 360 (6 September 2001): 26–28.

INTERVIEWS

Dawn Benander, Terra Museum

Ron Bloomfield, Bay Country (WI) Historical Museum

Stasha Boyd, Q Media Productions, Inc.

C. J. Brafford, Ute Indian Museum

Megan Evans, Liberty Hall Historic Site

Joseph Fazzino, Mark Twain House and Museum

Emily Stearns Fertik, Wenham Museum

Jay Finney, Museum of Contemporary Photography, Columbia College Chicago

Cristin Grant, Susan B. Anthony House

Thomas Hamilton, Professor of Marketing

Richard Hayes, Architect

Jerome Johnson, Executive Director, Garfield Farms, LaFox, IL

Bernard Kapuza, Professor of Advertising Design and Graphics

Roberta Gray Katz, Professor of Art History

Erika Kent, Ten Chimneys

Ruth Lasky, Museum Consultant

Laura Lee, Boulder History Museum

Julie Marie Lemon, Museum of Contemporary Art, Chicago

Joan Leuenberger, Vesterheim Norwegian-American Museum

Lynne Loftis, Ella Sharp Museum

Jill MacKenzie, Hagley Museum and Library

A. B. Mifflin, Director, Illinois Central History Society, and Associate Editor, *Green Diamond* magazine

Starr Mitchell, Historic Arkansas Museum

Cherie Newell, Oakland Museum of California

Patricia Rath, Professsor of Merchandising

Elizabeth Safanda, Preservation Partners, St. Charles, IL

Bill Shanahan, Professor of Advertising

Louise Terzia, Historic Arkansas Museum

Jane Textor, Director, Wilmette Historical Museum

John Textor, President, Wilmette Historical Museum

Gary Thatcher, Chicago Cultural Center

Susan Trien, Strong Museum

Karen Visser, Kalamazoo (MI) Valley Museum

Caitlin Von Schmidt, Heritage Harbor Museum

Jocelyn Young, Anchorage Museum of History and Art

Index

About the Author

Margot A. Wallace is professor of marketing communication at Columbia College Chicago, where she teaches a course in branding. A former creative director at J. Walter Thompson Advertising, a major global advertising agency, she has created branded campaigns for clients ranging from breakfast cereal to banks to colleges. For eight years, Professor Wallace served on the women's board of the Museum of Contemporary Art in Chicago.